A Note From Rick Renner

I am on a personal quest to see a "revival of the Bible" so people can establish their lives on a firm foundation that will stand strong and endure the test as the end-time storm winds begin to intensify.

In order to experience a revival of the Bible in your personal life, it is important to take time each day to read, receive, and apply its truths to your life. James tells us that if we will continue in the perfect law of liberty — refusing to be forgetful hearers but determined to be doers — we will be blessed in our ways. As you watch or listen to the programs in this series and work through this corresponding study guide, I trust that you will search the Scriptures and allow the Holy Spirit to help you hear something new from God's Word that applies specifically to your life. I encourage you to be a doer of the Word that He reveals to you. Whatever the cost, I assure you — it will be worth it.

Thy words were found, and I did eat them;
and thy word was unto me the joy and rejoicing of mine heart:
for I am called by thy name, O Lord God of hosts.
—Jeremiah 15:16

Your brother and friend in Jesus Christ,

Rick Renner

Christ's Message to Pergamum

1814 W. Tacoma St.
Broken Arrow, OK 74012-1406

Published by Rick Renner Ministries
www.renner.org

ISBN 13: 978-1-68031-617-9

eBook ISBN 13: 978-1-68031-655-1

How To Use This Study Guide

This ten-lesson study guide corresponds to ***"Christ's Message to Pergamum" With Rick Renner*** **(Renner TV)**. Each lesson in this study guide covers a topic that is addressed during the program series, with questions and references supplied to draw you deeper into your own private study of the Scriptures on this subject.

To derive the most benefit from this study guide, consider the following:

First, watch or listen to the program prior to working through the corresponding lesson in this guide. (Programs can also be viewed at **renner.org** by clicking on the Media/Archives links or on our Renner Ministries YouTube channel.)

Second, take the time to look up the scriptures included in each lesson. Prayerfully consider their application to your own life.

Third, use a journal or notebook to make note of your answers to each lesson's Study Questions and Practical Application challenges.

Fourth, invest specific time in prayer and in the Word of God to consult with the Holy Spirit. Write down the scriptures or insights He reveals to you.

Finally, take action! Whatever the Lord tells you to do according to His Word, do it.

For added insights on this subject, it is recommended that you obtain Rick Renner's book ***No Room for Compromise: A Light in Darkness, Volume Two***. You can also select from Rick's other available resources by placing your order at **renner.org** or by calling 1-800-742-5593.

LESSON 1

TOPIC

The City of Pergamum

SCRIPTURES

1. **Revelation 2:12** — And to the angel of the church in Pergamos write; These things saith he which hath the sharp sword with two edges.
2. **Revelation 2:12 (*RIV*)** — I am the One who ultimately holds the sharp sword with two edges. Regardless of the power any human leader may temporarily try to exert over your lives, I am the One who has the final say in matters of life and death.
3. **Revelation 2:13** — I know thy works, and where thou dwellest, even where Satan's seat is: and thou holdest fast my name, and hast not denied my faith, even in those days wherein Antipas was my faithful martyr, who was slain among you, where Satan dwelleth.
4. **John 1:5 (*NKJV*)** — And the light shines in the darkness, and the darkness did not comprehend it.

GREEK WORDS

1. "comprehended"— μ (*katalambano*): to seize; to grab hold of; to pull down; to tackle; to conquer; to master; to hold under one's power
2. "angel"— (*angelos*): a human messenger or an angel; one sent on a special mission; one dispatched to perform a specific assignment; a delegate or dignitary; pictures the role of a pastor; a messenger of God
3. "church"— (*ekklesia*): a called, separated, and prestigious assembly; a prestigious assembly of distinguished citizens who determined laws, debated public policy, formulated new policies, argued and ruled in judicial matters, elected chief magistrates, and decided who should be banished; a body of believers who have been called out, called forth, selected, and assembled to be God's representatives in every town, city, state or nation; a body called to make decisions that affect the atmosphere of a region

4. “sharp sword”— μ (*rhomphaia*): a sharp, sickle-shaped blade affixed to a long pole; it was known for its long reach and its ability to cut through thick armor; its back-and-forth hacking motion, similar to that of a farmer using a sickle, penetrated the tightly packed formation of enemies
5. “right of the sword”— (Latin, *jus gladii*): the equivalent to what we call the power of life and death, referring to the legal authority to execute someone for a capital offense
6. “I know”— (*oida*): to see, perceive, understand, or comprehend; pictures knowledge gained by personal experience or personal observation
7. “works”— (*erga*): deeds, actions, or activities
8. “dwellest”— (*katoikeo*): to settle down; pictures one who has settled into a house and feels completely at home there; the verb tense indicates continuous action

SYNOPSIS

Pergamum was one of the seven cities mentioned by the apostle John in the opening chapters of the book of Revelation. This city was filled with temples where sacrifices were being offered to pagan gods. Spiritually, it was very dark, literally teeming with demon spirits and abounding in mysterious and evil religions. The population surrounding the church at Pergamum was primarily comprised of pagans who misunderstood the new Christian faith. Christians were being persecuted and great pressure was upon them to compromise their faith in order to live peaceably with their pagan neighbors.

Pergamum is a perfect example of the power and ability of the Gospel to penetrate any environment. In the midst of a greatly oppressive atmosphere in which the church was viciously persecuted, *the church not only survived — it thrived!*

During this time, there was a teaching called the doctrine of the Nicolaitans, which reasoned, “What harm is there in making a few compromises to be more like our pagan neighbors? Why not enter their pagan temples or burn a little incense to their gods? If it will provide us with peace with them, perhaps accommodating the people around us would be beneficial.”

As the believers in Pergamum began to succumb to this reasoning and compromise, Jesus spoke to them in Revelation 2:16, saying, “Repent.”

He commanded them to change — to stop making room for compromise and to do the right thing in the presence of God regardless of the consequences.

Repentance is part of the Christian life, both then and now. It is important to know what the Bible teaches about repentance and to understand what it actually means.

The focus of this lesson is Christ's message to the church in Pergamum. You may think, *Pergamum? What relevance is that to me?* But as we complete this study, you will be amazed at how this important message is timeless and relevant for believers in the Church today.

The ten lessons in this study, ***Christ's Message to Pergamum***, will focus on the following topics:

- The City of Pergamum
- What Is the Seat of Satan?
- Antipas, Jesus' Beloved Martyr
- Who Is Balaam?
- Balaam and His Doctrine — Part 1
- Balaam and His Doctrine — Part 2
- Who Are the Nicolaitans?
- Do Christians Ever Need To Repent?
- Christ's Sword and Divine Judgment
- A Message to Overcomers

The emphasis of this lesson:

Regardless of the darkness that may be surrounding individual believers and the Church today, just as it was in the church in Pergamum, "Darkness does not have the ability to suppress or to hold the light under its domain" (John 1:5 *RIV*).

Pergamum, a City of Sophistication

Pergamum was a magnificent city on the western side of the Roman province of Asia. Located the farthest north of the seven churches mentioned in the book of Revelation, it sat on the crest of a hill and was simply amazing in appearance! The city was intentionally created to mirror Athens, which was considered one of the most sophisticated cities of the Western world at that time.

In many ways Pergamum excelled over Athens in its architecture, sculpture and art, education, and philosophers of renown. However, the city was teeming with idols and pagan temples. In fact, it was viewed as the epicenter of idolatry during the First Century.

John stated in Revelation 2:12 and 13, "And to the angel of the church in Pergamos write; These things saith he which hath the sharp sword with two edges. I know thy works, and where thou dwellest, even where Satan's seat is: and thou holdest fast my name, and hast not denied my faith, even in those days wherein Antipas was my faithful martyr, who was slain among you, where Satan dwelleth."

Twice in this passage Jesus stated that Satan dwelled in Pergamum. In the entire Roman Empire, no city was more engrossed in idolatry and paganism than the city of Pergamum!

Even 300 years after the writings of the New Testament, Pergamum continued to be completely engaged in occult rituals and idolatry. In fact, one Roman emperor who had been raised as a Christian defected from the faith and decided to become a devout pagan. To give you an idea of the widespread notoriety of this darkened city, to facilitate his conversion and devotion to paganism, this emperor packed his bags and moved to Pergamum!

The Church Is Born and a Great Light Penetrates the Darkness!

The darkest religious site in the entire city of Pergamum was the Great Altar of Zeus. It was gilded in gold and covered with magnificent frescos. Today this altar can be seen in the city of Berlin at the Pergamum Museum. Created nearly 3,000 years ago, it is a breathtaking and monumental sculpture.

The Altar of Zeus was just one of the many temples and altars in the city of Pergamum. Twenty-four hours a day, smoke from the sacrifices offered to pagan gods billowed into the sky, literally hovering over the acropolis of Pergamum. With smoke surging into the air and the gold on the Altar of Zeus shining in the light of the sun, it must have been a spectacular sight for visitors approaching the city from the valley below.

Although Pergamum was beautiful outwardly, spiritually it was one of the darkest places in the entire Roman Empire. Yet, amidst all that darkness, the Church of our Lord Jesus Christ was born! Where sin abounds, grace much more abounds (*see* Romans 5:20)! Wherever darkness and sin are abundant, God loves to pour out His supernatural grace. And that is *precisely* what God did in the city of Pergamum when the Church was birthed in the midst of deep spiritual darkness.

He Who Held the Sword

The city of Pergamum was also the headquarters for the proconsul of Rome. The proconsul was the highest authority in the entire Roman province of Asia. He was a judge, a governor, an executor, and had the final say in all things pertaining to the law.

In the city of Pergamum, the proconsul sat on a throne and had the authority to determine who would live or die. He was given what was known in Latin as *jus gladii*, or *right of the sword.* In other words, if the proconsul dropped the sword, it meant execution was imminent. Life could be extended or extinguished depending on how the sword was held. His power was so weighty that his decisions not only affected Pergamum, but whatever he ultimately ruled in a matter would be extended over the entire province.

Believers in Pergamum were living under the shadow of that sword. Because of their Christian faith and because they would not worship the emperor, the proconsul opposed them. Christians in Pergamum were in constant danger because of the Roman proconsul who held the sword.

Pushing Back the Darkness

By the time the church was birthed in Pergamum, the city was already very old. For at least 400 years before the First Century, pagans had been coming from all over the Roman Empire to conduct ritual occult sacrifices in Pergamum. With sacrificial smoke consuming the air, eerie music emanating from temples, and detestable sexual acts occurring throughout the city, it would seem a very unlikely setting for the inception of the church in Pergamum.

Although it cannot be proven, it is likely that the church of Pergamum began during Paul's three-year residence in the city of Ephesus. While he resided in that city, churches were birthed all over Asia, and it was a very exciting time for the Gospel.

A powerful political city, Pergamum was less than 100 miles from Ephesus. What happened in Pergamum would eventually spread to all of the cities in Asia. Paul was very strategic in everything he did. It is very likely Paul's desire would have been to reach the city of Pergamum with the Gospel, knowing the result would prove to be positive throughout the entire continent of Asia.

Whether Paul traveled to Pergamum himself or dispatched teams from Ephesus to Pergamum, he became the apostle to the church in Pergamum. When the Gospel arrived in that city, something truly amazing transpired: *It pushed back the powers of darkness!* The light of the Gospel began to penetrate the dark spiritual environment in Pergamum.

John 1:5 says, "And the light shineth in darkness; and the darkness comprehended it not." The word "comprehended" is the Greek word *katalambano*, which means *to seize*, *to grab hold of*, *to pull down*, *to tackle*, *to conquer*, *to master*, or *to hold under one's power*.

The *Renner's Interpretive Version* (*RIV*) of John 1:5 says, "Darkness does not have the ability to suppress or to hold the light under its domain." This verse triumphantly declares that darkness is ultimately incapable of suppressing the light or holding it under its domain. Darkness *always* surrenders as light breaks through with all its glorious brilliance!

In the midst of the intense oppression in the city of Pergamum, people began to be evangelized. God's people started to grow spiritually, and the light of the Gospel began to *blaze* in that city! However, it was not without opposition from the devil. Inhumane persecution eventually came to the Church, and living in an environment where Satan thrived, believers contended with bullying, persecution, prejudice, and imprisonment. Many were even martyred for their faith. But in the midst of it all, they did not surrender, but continued to shine as lights in the darkness!

Darkness may seem to be powerful, but it simply does not have the power to master the light of the Gospel. Darkness always crumbles — it always fades — when the Gospel light is preached. From the very beginning of the Church, evil has tried to suppress the light, but the enemy's efforts have been unsuccessful because the light of God *always* prevails, even in the bleakest and most gloomy circumstances. The same is true for *your* life. If you will embrace and believe it, the Gospel — the Word of God — can prevail over any dark situation you may be facing right now.

Who Was the Angel of the Church in Pergamum?

Revelation 2:12 begins, "And to the angel of the church in Pergamum write these things...."

The word "angel" is the same word Jesus used to address the churches of Ephesus and Smyrna. It is the Greek word *angelos*. This word "angel" does not necessarily describe a heavenly angel with wings that can fly. The Greek word *angelos* portrays *a human messenger*, *delegate*, or *dignitary*; *one sent on a special mission, one dispatched to perform a specific assignment*. It depicts the role of a pastor — a messenger of God — in this case, the pastor of the church in Pergamum.

When Jesus had something to say to the church of Pergamum, He didn't directly address the church. He addressed the pastor of that work. This is important because God never bypasses the authority He has set in place. God respects those in authority, and so should we. If God has something positive to say to a local church, He will first speak to the pastor. If God has correction to give to a church, the pastor will be the first to hear it from the Supreme Head of the Church. It is then the pastor's responsibility to assimilate what the Lord has spoken and deliver it to the congregation in the power of the Holy Spirit. That is one function of the pastor.

The Church — God's 'Ruling Body' in the Earth

In Revelation 2:12, Christ honors the pastor of the church and says, "And to the angel of the church in Pergamum write these things...." The word "church" is the Greek word *ekklesia*, and it is a very well-known word from Greek society. Originally, this was a very political word describing *a called, separated, prestigious assembly of distinguished citizens who determined laws, debated public policy, formulated new policies, and argued and ruled in judicial matters*. They decided who should be banished if necessary and who should be elected, etc.

When used in the context of the Church, *ekklesia* describes *a body of believers who have been called out, called forth, selected, and assembled to be God's representative in every town, every city, every state, and every nation*. It is God's people assembled together to make decisions affecting the atmosphere of a region. The meaning of the word "church" is *an assembled body of believers, or an assembled group, that has power to make decisions that affect a city, a state, or a nation to change an environment.*

God's intention is for the Church to be a people with the power to change the world! We are God's prophetic voice wherever we are. God never intended for the church be a fearful, cowardly, hidden group of people with no motivation to contest or reign over spiritual darkness in the world around them. His plan is for the Church to rise to a position of power and influence. The Greek word for "church" — *ekklesia* — emphatically defines this role.

Because of persecution, believers in Pergamum were struggling to fulfill their place as the "Church" — the *ekkesia.* During that time, the Emperor Domitian was in power. Domitian hated the Church, hated believers, and wanted to extinguish the Christian faith. As a result, the church in Pergamum was an underground church for a time because of intense persecution, but they operated in spiritual power that began to change the atmosphere of their city.

Regardless of how dark the circumstances were or the struggles the Pergamene believers faced because of opposing powers, when Jesus addressed the church in Pergamum, He still called them "the Church." They were His "called out ones," separated to rule and reign in the power of the Gospel. The same is true for us today.

STUDY QUESTIONS

Study to shew thyself approved unto God, a workman that needeth not to be ashamed, rightly dividing the word of truth.
— 2 Timothy 2:15

1. The church in Pergamum was birthed in the midst of great spiritual darkness, where pagan worship transpired 24 hours a day. According to Romans 5:20 and Romans 6:14, explain how "birth" was possible.
2. Although darkness may seem powerful against the light of the Gospel, explain why it is powerless according to John 1:5.
3. Who was the "angel" of the Pergamum church referred to in Revelation chapter 2? What is the significance of this position? How does this relate to the *ekklesia* — the Church — including *local churches* in every city, state, and nation?

PRACTICAL APPLICATION

But be ye doers of the word, and not hearers only, deceiving your own selves.
—James 1:22

1. We have been given the Word of God and the Spirit of God as weapons against the darkness surrounding us. What steps can you take in your life to guard against the darkness of today's culture according to Romans 12:2 and Romans 13:13?
2. Examine your heart to determine if you have been tempted to be critical of your local pastor? If so, ask God to forgive you. Look up the following passages and write a list of reasons you should support the pastor of your local church: First Timothy 2:1-3, Hebrews 13:7, and Philippians 2: 3, 4.

LESSON 2

TOPIC

What Is the Seat of Satan?

SCRIPTURES

1. **Revelation 2:12** — And to the angel of the church in Pergamum write; These things saith he which hath the sharp sword with two edges.
2. **Revelation 2:13** — I know thy works, and where thou dwellest, even where Satan's seat is: and thou holdest fast my name, and hast not denied my faith, even in those days wherein Antipas was my faithful martyr, who was slain among you, where Satan dwelleth.
3. **Revelation 2:13 (*RIV*)** — From my personal observation of you, I know about all of your activities. I have seen it all. I know all there is to know. In fact, there is nothing about you or your works that I do not know....
4. **Ephesians 6:12** — For we wrestle not against flesh and blood, but against principalities, against powers, against the rulers of the darkness of this world, against spiritual wickedness in high places.

5. **Revelation 2:13 (*RIV*)** — ...When you had the opportunity to break your vow and walk away, you did not do it....

GREEK WORDS

1. "I know" — (*oida*): to see, perceive, understand, or comprehend; pictures knowledge gained by personal experience or personal observation
2. "works" — (*erga*): deeds, actions, or activities
3. "dwellest" — (*katoikeo*): to settle down; pictures one who has settled into a house and feels completely at home there; the verb tense indicates continuous action
4. "Satan" — (*Satanas*): one who hates, accuses, slanders, or conspires against; an adversary
5. "seat" — (*thronos*): the earliest use described physical chairs in people's homes that were reserved solely for the head of a household; in ancient times, the man of the house held supreme authority over all domestic matters, and he had the final say-so in all decisions or business transactions that might affect his family; it was customary to refer to the head of the house as "lord" of his home, so a seat was designated to represent the high rank of the man of the house within his family; it was considered inappropriate and disrespectful for anyone else to sit in his place of honor; a seat for the undisputed master of his house, and that seat was a symbol of his ultimate authority; in eastern lands of the Roman Empire, pagans used the word *thronos* to describe invisible seats of power upon which the local or patron gods or goddesses sat to rule their towns, cities, or provinces
6. "holdest fast" — (*kratos*): pictures a powerful grip; to seize, take hold of, firmly grip, or apprehend; these believers were holding tightly to the name of Jesus because demonic powers were trying to wrench it from their hands. The fact that Jesus used this word affirms pressures of all sorts — religious, cultural, social, and political — were being levied against the Christians in this city. But they made a decision to *hold tight* and *to retain* their commitment to Jesus Christ, no matter what price was required of them
7. "denied" — μ (*arneomai*): to deny, disown, reject, refuse, or renounce; commonly referred to a person who had become unfaithful in a relationship and subsequently disavowed, forsook, walked away from, and washed one's hands of that other person; the motive for

denial was usually fear of others, fear of suffering ridicule or persecution, or anxiety about what others would think

8. "my faith"— ϖ μ (*ten pistin mou*): the faith; a specific set of beliefs or a specific doctrine, creed, or faith; when *mou* is used in conjunction with the phrase *ten pistin*, an accurate translation could read *my faith*, *the faith that belongs to me*, or *the faith that I hold closely*.

SYNOPSIS

The Great Altar of Zeus, located in the ancient city of Pergamum, was so magnificent, it was considered one of the seven wonders of the ancient world. But Pergamum was such a wicked city that twice in Revelation 2:13, Jesus referred to it as "the seat of Satan."

The Greek word for "seat" in this passage is *thronos*. The English word for "throne" is derived from it. Satan not only ruled the city of Pergamum from this high and lofty citadel or stronghold, but he also ruled the entire province of Asia through authorities that were located in Pergamum.

Believers in Pergamum were constantly confronted with evil. They could not escape it. As they walked through the streets of the city, the presence of the Altar of Zeus and the smoke of the burning incense rising from it were unavoidable. Believers could not escape the presence of evil, but rather than yield to it, the Pergamum believers learned how to resist and overcome it. They learned to refrain from the evil surrounding them and instead, practiced living holy and separated lives by walking in the power of the Holy Spirit. And they did so victoriously!

Since the believers in Pergamum — surrounded by evil in the city where the very "seat of Satan" dwelt — could live holy, powerful, and passionate lives before God, we, too, can resist evil in our day and walk in the power and victory found in Jesus Christ!

The emphasis of this lesson:

We may be living in the most seriously challenging time the Church has confronted in more than 1,700 years. It is vital to know how to navigate through the days that lie before us. The Early Church in Pergamum can teach us how to traverse even the darkest seasons of our personal lives. The Pergamene believers did it, *and so can we!*

Called Out, Not Hidden

In Revelation 2:12, Jesus addressed the leadership of the church. He spoke to the "angel" or the pastor of the church when He said, "And to the angel of the church in Pergamum write; these things saith he which hath the sharp sword with two edges; I know where thou dwellest, even where Satan's seat is; and thou holdest fast my name, and hath not denied my faith, even in those days wherein Antipas was my martyr, who was slain among you, where Satan dwelleth."

As we noted in our previous lesson, the word for "church" in this verse was very political. The Greek word, *ekklesia*, is comprised of two words; *ek*, which means *out*, and *kaleo*, which means *to call*. When you compound these two words, *ekklesia* means *called out ones.*

When *ekklesia* is used to describe the Church, it depicts a body called upon by God to make decisions that affect the atmosphere of a region. God never intended for the Church to be a reclusive group of believers hiding from the world. God has called us to rise to a place of influence and power. We have been called out to change the environment where we have been placed. The word *ekklesia* or "church" emphatically expressed God's intended purpose for His people.

Jesus Knows Us by Personal Observation

Revelation 2:13 begins, "I know thy works...." The word "know" is the Greek word *oida*. The word *oida* always describes firsthand knowledge. This is not hearsay information or something that's reported by an angel or by someone in prayer; it means *to see and observe it with your own eyes.* This Greek word for "know" — *oida* — literally means *to see, perceive, understand or comprehend by personal observation.*

In Revelation chapters 1 and 2, we are told that Jesus was walking in the midst of the church and as He walked, He was *observing* and *watching.* Jesus was literally *seeing, perceiving, understanding, comprehending, and gaining knowledge of the church by personal experience or observation.*

We should consider this both an encouragement and a warning. It should encourage us that Jesus is aware of everything happening in the Church and in our lives. When the church of Pergamum received this message, it must have been a great encouragement to learn that Jesus understood the very bleak environment that surrounded them.

In a similar way, this should also serve as a warning because Jesus sees and knows everything firsthand. Jesus sees every victory won, but also every misstep taken. Jesus also saw every challenge faced by the believers in the church at Pergamum. He saw every demonic attack they withstood along with every error they tolerated. He saw it all.

This word "know" emphatically means Christ unequivocally possessed knowledge about the church of Pergamum based on His own personal observation. He viewed every aspect of the church and knew its condition because He had seen it with his own eyes.

What Jesus Knew

Jesus knew many things about the church of Pergamum, but we will examine three. First, He knew about the demonic environment in which they lived. He understood the opposition coming against them.

Second, He knew they lived under the sword of the proconsul. The believers in Pergamum lived under the dreaded *"right of the sword,"* which could be used to determine whether they were permitted to live or sentenced to die.

Third, Jesus knew they were living under dreadful circumstances — being assailed by pagans from without. Jesus had knowledge of what these believers encountered daily.

Hebrews 13:8 says, "Jesus Christ the same yesterday, and to day, and for ever." This means what Jesus *did* is what He *does.* Since Jesus was walking among the churches then, He is walking among us now. Since Jesus was observing the church then, He is observing us now. Since Jesus was looking at *their* victories, He is also looking at *our* victories. Since Jesus was looking at their error, He is looking at how we tolerate error too.

Jesus does today exactly what He was doing 2,000 years ago. He is the same *yesterday, today, and forever.*

Hebrews 4:13 says, "…All things are naked and opened unto the eyes of him with whom we have to do." Jesus sees it all, so let's be determined that He will have pleasure in what He sees in our lives and in our churches.

Jesus Knows It All

Revelation 2:13 continues, "I know thy works…." The word "works" is the Greek word *erga*, which describes *deeds*, *actions*, or *activities*.

The *Renner's Interpretive Version* (*RIV*) of Revelation 2:13 expresses best the meaning of this word "works": "From my personal observation of you, I know all about your activities. I've seen it all. I know all there is to know. In fact, there's nothing about you or your works that I do not know."

It is interesting to note that Jesus said *"I know thy works"* to all seven of the churches mentioned in the book of Revelation. Jesus knew about every one of them. And Jesus knows about *you*. He knows about your church. He knows about the church down the street. He knows because He walks in the church with open eyes. He is observing.

For example, in Revelation 2:4, Jesus said the church of Ephesus was a hard-working church that had lost its first love. How did He know that? He was in the church. Jesus knew that from observation.

In Revelation 2:9, Jesus described the church in Smyrna. He knew they were facing poverty and tribulation. How did He know? Because He had been there, and He knew it firsthand for Himself.

In Revelation 2:13, Jesus knew the church of Pergamum was living under the political shadow of the Roman governor, experiencing political and spiritual pressures, and enduring deadly persecution. He had personally been there and had seen it.

In Revelation 2:19 and 20, Jesus knew the church at Thyatira had done many good works, but they were in jeopardy because of false doctrine that was trying to infiltrate their ranks.

In Revelation 3:2, Jesus described the church at Sardis. He had been in the church at Sardis, and with His own eyes observed that they had a great reputation outwardly, but spiritually they were about to die.

Jesus had also been in the church of Philadelphia. We read about that in Revelation 3:8. Jesus could see they had a great open door — many opportunities for preaching the Gospel.

Jesus had also been in the church of Laodicea, which was a very prosperous church. Jesus said to them in Revelation 3:16, "I know you're rich and you're increased with goods, but spiritually you're lukewarm. You have grown cold concerning the things of God."

Jesus knew intimate details about each of the seven churches listed in the book of Revelation. He did not repeat the same observations to every church. He knew each church so specifically, so individually, that He could address unique characteristics in every one of them.

Jesus Christ has not changed! What does Jesus know about you? What does He know about your church? *He knows everything!*

Satan's Seat '*Unseated*'

In Revelation 2:13, Jesus continues by saying, "I know thy works, and where thou dwellest, even where Satan's seat is...." The word "dwellest" is very important. It is the Greek word *katoikeo*, meaning *to settle down*. The word depicts one who is settled into a house or neighborhood. This individual feels completely at home. The verb tense for "dwellest" describes continuous action. In other words, this is not a visitor or guest who is coming and going. The Greek word *katoikeo* indicates *permanent indwellers*.

This was especially important to the believers in Pergamum whom Jesus was addressing. They were suffering dire persecution and could not escape their environment. Everyone would like to escape hardship, but there are times when it is not possible. In that day, citizens of the Roman Empire were required to live where the government dictated. The believers in Pergamum were legally obligated to live there because that was where the government gave them permission and the right to live. Generations of families had lived in Pergamum. This was the place where they *regularly dwelled*, and Jesus fully understood that they could not flee their situation.

When Jesus said to them, "I know where you dwell," the Greek could actually be translated, "I know where you've settled down and where you continually dwell — it's the place where Satan's seat is."

When Jesus referred to "Satan's seat," He used the Greek word *satanas* for Satan. This word describes *one who hates, accuses, or slanders* or *one who conspires against another as an adversary*. This reveals that Satan was conspiring against the church at Pergamum. He was not haphazardly hoping to destroy the church there. He had a plan to do it!

Again, Revelation 2:13 says, "I know where you dwell, even where Satan's seat is." The word "seat" is the Greek word *thronos*. The earliest use of this word described *physical chairs in people's homes that were reserved solely for the head of a household*.

In ancient times, the man of the house held supreme authority over all domestic matters and had the final say in all decisions. It was customary to refer to the head of the house as the "lord of the house." He had a seat specifically designated for him, and no one else was permitted to sit in that seat. It was exclusively for the master of the house, and it was considered highly inappropriate and disrespectful for anyone else to sit in his place of honor. His seat was a symbol of his ultimate authority.

In Pergamum and other eastern lands of the Roman Empire, pagans commonly used this word *thronos* to describe *invisible seats of power upon which the local gods sat to rule their towns, cities, or provinces.*

By using this word *thronos* or "seat," Jesus was saying that in Pergamum, Satan was the master of the house. He had a throne upon which he sat. He was the absolute ruler of the "house" in Pergamum. Satan had ruled there for generations with no resistance. He had previously had free reign. Satan's power was so entrenched in the city through the authority of the Roman government established there that he began to rule the whole region of Asia. That reign absolutely blanketed the area with spiritual darkness. Satan's power had been unchallenged in Pergamum and surrounding areas for centuries.

However, once the church was birthed in Pergamum, Satan's seat became threatened, and his power was confronted and challenged by the new believers in Christ in that city. The church was driving back darkness. They were determined to unseat Satan in their city.

When the Bible refers to the "the seat of Satan," it is very important to notice the use of a definite article in Greek. The reason this is important is, it is describing a specific throne — an *actual throne or seat*! Satan was seated on a real seat in Pergamum! And Jesus was calling on the church to unseat him.

Jesus is calling us to do the same today. He is calling us to unseat Satan in our families, communities, cities, states, regions, and nations! God doesn't want the devil to be the master of the house.

You have been equipped by God with His Word, His power, and the blood of Jesus Christ! That is how powerful you are! If you will choose to preach the Gospel and shine its glorious light, you will push the darkness out, too, and unseat Satan from his previously held territory. That was Christ's message to the church of Pergamum, and it is His message for the Church, the Body of Christ, today.

STUDY QUESTIONS

Study to shew thyself approved unto God, a workman that needeth not to be ashamed, rightly dividing the word of truth.
— 2 Timothy 2:15

1. Study Jesus' words in John 17:14-20. Jesus prayed not that God would remove us from the world, but that He would keep us from the evil one. What powerful weapon found in this passage has been provided to every believer? List three ways you are using this weapon in your life today.
2. Explain the original meaning of *ekklesia* and God's intended purpose for His church. As "the light of the world" (Matthew 5:14-16) and an "ambassador for Christ" (2 Corinthians 5:20), what are some practical ways you can fulfill God's original purpose for His Church?

PRACTICAL APPLICATION

But be ye doers of the word, and not hearers only, deceiving your own selves.
— James 1:22

1. Take time to examine your heart today. Are there areas you can identify where the enemy has attempted to "settle down" to dwell? Maybe he has tried to permanently take over your healing, your prosperity, or your relationships? What weapons from God's Word will you employ to "dethrone" him in your life today?

LESSON 3

TOPIC

Antipas, Jesus' Beloved Martyr

SCRIPTURES

1. **Revelation 2:12** — And to the angel of the church in Pergamum write; These things saith he which hath the sharp sword with two edges.

2. **Revelation 2:13** — I know thy works, and where thou dwellest, even where Satan's seat is: and thou holdest fast my name, and hast not denied my faith, even in those days wherein Antipas was my faithful martyr, who was slain among you, where Satan dwelleth.
3. **Revelation 2:13 (*RIV*)** — ...When you had the opportunity to break your vow and walk away, you did not do it....

GREEK WORDS

1. "holdest fast" — (*kratos*): pictures a powerful grip; to seize, take hold of, firmly grip, or apprehend; these believers were *holding tightly* to the name of Jesus and *retaining* their commitment to Him because demonic powers were trying to wrench it from their hands
2. "denied" — μ (*arneomai*): to deny, disown, reject, refuse, or renounce; commonly referred to a person who had become unfaithful in a relationship and subsequently disavowed, forsook, walked away from, and washed one's hands of that other person; the motive for denial was usually fear of others, fear of suffering ridicule or persecution, or anxiety about what others would think
3. "my faith" — ϖ μ (*ten pistin mou*): the faith; a specific set of beliefs or a specific doctrine, creed, or faith; when *mou* is used in conjunction with the phrase *ten pistin*, an accurate translation could read *my faith*, *the faith that belongs to me*, or *the faith that I hold closely*
4. "my faithful martyr" — μ μ ϖ (*ho martus mou ho pistos*)

   "my martyr" — μ μ (*ho martus*): a witness summoned to testify in a court of law; the evidence or proof presented in a legal case; pictures a legal witness who was only allowed to speak what he personally knew to be true; depicts the personal insight that qualified a person to be a "witness" worthy of being put on a public stand for examination; was also connected to the idea of suffering because if a person was called to be a witness, he was required to be faithful to the truth regardless of any potential acts of retribution that might be carried out against him by those who opposed his witness or who wished to suppress the truth; when an individual was summoned to be a "witness," it was understood that it could place him or his loved ones in jeopardy; to be a "witness" required the highest level of integrity and commitment, as well as a willingness to sacrifice oneself or one's status to uphold the truth; it was a very real possibility that a person could pay a high price for being a *faithful* witness

5. "my faithful martyr"— μ μ ϖ (*ho martus mou ho pistos*)

   "faithful"— ϖ μ (*ho pistos*): faithfulness or trustworthiness; could be translated "the faithful one" or "the trustworthy one"; in context, Christ found him to be faithful and trustworthy in spite of the agonizing circumstances that challenged him
6. "slain"— ϖ (*apokteino*): to slay or to kill; pictures the abrupt taking away of a person's life — in other words, murder, execution, or mass killing; violent death; butchery; carnage; a brutal, grisly, and gruesome death
7. "among you"— ϖ ' μ (*par humin*): right alongside you, or in your very midst; Antipas was martyred in a public, visible location, where the entire city would have been made aware of this hideous event
8. "Satan"— (*Satanas*): one who hates, accuses, slanders, or conspires against; an adversary
9. "dwellest"— (*katoikeo*): to settle down; pictures one who has settled into a house and feels completely at home there; the verb tense indicates continuous action

SYNOPSIS

The city of Pergamum was a very oppressive place, filled with demonic powers and all types of dark, mysterious pagan religions. In the center of the city lived a Christian leader named Antipas. He had created quite a ruckus in the city because he was casting demons out of people who had been tormented and controlled by them. The pagans in Pergamum became agitated, claiming the demons were upset because Antipas was casting them out. Antipas simply exercised his authority through Jesus Christ over demon spirits, and the pagans became so angry about it they took their complaint to the governor who resided in the acropolis. They implored the governor, in effect saying, "Do something about this Christian man, Antipas, who is casting out devils!"

The governor summoned Antipas for a trial. Early records indicate that when Antipas stood before the governor, he was commanded to repent of casting out demons and to return to his pagan roots. But Antipas refused and was martyred as a consequence.

Jesus referred to this in Revelation 2:13 when He concretely describes Antipas as "*My faithful martyr who was slain.*"

The Greek word for "slain" is *apokteino*, and it is the word for *carnage* or *butchery*. History records that there was a brazen bull in the acropolis of Pergamum. It was made of metal and was hollow inside. In the head area of this metal bull, pipes had been placed and "music" or sound could emanate from them. There was also a side door where victims were placed to burn them alive as a fire was ignited beneath the brazen bull.

This is what happened to Antipas. They placed him inside this bronze bull, lit a fire, and closed the door. As the fire began to heat up, the metal became hot and Antipas was literally fried to death. Through the musical pipes in the head of the statue, the screams of victims like Antipas made it seem like the bull was alive. This was a horrific death, and when the pagans later opened the doors where victims had been burned, the pagans would extract and polish the bones to wear as jewelry.

Some people suggest Antipas did not exist, but Jesus called him by name in Revelation 2:13, and his life and death can inspire believers today to hold on to the name of Jesus, to not conform to outside pressure, and to refuse to deny the faith.

The emphasis of this lesson:

Although Antipas was surrounded by the permeating darkness in Pergamum, he was not intimidated by the demonic influences of the godless culture, nor the persecution confronting him. Instead, he continued to allow the light of God that penetrates the darkness of Satan to shine brightly through his life as he lived boldly for the Lord.

The Gospel Will Unseat Satan

In a very real sense, the believers in Pergamum were dealing with spiritual principalities. Paul states in Ephesians 6:12, "For we wrestle not against flesh and blood, but against principalities...." In the city of Pergamum, a door had been opened so wide to the spirit realm in centuries past. Satan had come in like a flood and had established a seat of authority. Believers in the city could not escape the spiritual darkness because the entire atmosphere was filled with demonic activity. Satan had entered the region to establish a seat of authority, and like a flood, "*principalities, powers, rulers of darkness, and spiritual wickedness*" had entered Pergamum.

In those early days of the Church, the light had just begun penetrating the darkness in Pergamum, and the Gospel was beginning to unseat Satan, the master of the house. The Gospel will do the same in your life, your family, your finances, your business, your church, and your neighborhood. *The Gospel will absolutely unseat Satan.*

Satan was greatly threatened by the newly emerging Church. Jesus commended the believers in Revelation 2:13, saying, in effect, "Even though you live in the city where Satan is seated, you have not denied Me, even after Antipas was martyred." The *King James Version* says, "...Thou holdest fast my name, and hast not denied my faith."

Continue To Hold Fast

The words "holdest fast" is the Greek word *kratos*. In this particular verse, it means *continually hold fast*, and it describes *a powerful grip*. The word *kratos* means *to seize*, *take hold of*, *firmly grip*, *or to apprehend*. The believers in Pergamum were holding tightly to the name of Jesus. They were wrapping their faith tightly around that name so that no one could take it from them.

Religious attacks, cultural attacks, social attacks, political attacks — all of these assaults were being levied against the Christians in Pergamum. Jesus' use of the word *kratos* — "holdest fast" — affirms the great pressures trying to wrench the name of Jesus from their hands. But those Christians had made a decision. They determined with firm, resolute resolve that they would *kratos* — hold tightly to the name of Jesus and would not allow anyone to tear it from their grip.

The Pergamene believers had made a decision *to hold tightly to* and *to retain* their commitment to Christ regardless of any price they had to pay. In spite of the pressure to surrender, to modify their faith, and to be more accommodating to the pagan worldview, they said, "We will *not* surrender! We will hold tightly to what has been declared to us. We will retain our commitment to Christ."

Jesus commended them in Revelation 2:13, saying, "...Thou holdest fast my name, and hast not denied my faith."

The word "denied" is the Greek word *arneomai* and means *to disown*, *to deny*, *to reject*, *to refuse*, or *to renounce.* It commonly referred to a person who became *unfaithful* in a relationship and subsequently *disavowed*, *forsook*, *walked away from, and washed his hands clean of that other person*. Fear was typically the motive for denial — fear of suffering, ridicule, persecution, or anxiety about the opinions of others. Based on those anxieties and fears, people would disavow their faith. They would walk away, wash their hands, and break their commitments to protect themselves from emotional or physical injury.

Revelation 2:13 could be translated, "*When you had the opportunity to break your vow and walk away, you did not do it.*" The church in Pergamum was amazing. Under extreme pressure, they refused to renounce the name of Jesus. The Pergamum believers remained faithful to the end. When given the opportunity to appease the pagans by denying the name of Jesus, they instead held fast to Christ.

'You Have Not Denied My Faith'

In verse 13, Jesus said, "...[Thou] hast not denied my faith...." The phrase "my faith" is very important. The Greek is *mou pistis*. The word *pistis* is the word for "faith," and *mou* means *me*, personalizing the meaning. This phrase could literally be translated as *the faith of Me*. The faith Jesus was referring to is not faith for miracles or even general faith. He was describing *the* faith, or the whole of faith in Him. In Greek, a definite article is used and expands this phrase to mean, "The creed we believe — the doctrines of the New Testament, those principles which are the foundation of Christianity — it is *mou*, or *mine*!"

The Greek meaning behind this verse conveys how deeply Jesus feels about the Christian faith. He calls it *His*. Jesus is saying, *"My faith, the faith that belongs to Me, the faith that I closely hold."* The Greek also shows both origination and possession, meaning the faith is *from* Christ, and it is *in the possession of* Christ. The Gospel not only comes from Christ, but it is still firmly in His possession. He is the Originator. He is the Giver. And He died for that faith. He knew that the believers in Pergamum were giving their lives for the right purpose and cause.

The early believers made the decision to hold tightly to the name of Jesus, and they would not break their commitment to *the* faith. The pressure to modify faith has existed from the inception of the Church Age. Pressure still exists today to dilute the faith to be more accommodating to the lost world. This is nothing new. *But don't do it!* It is not your faith, and you do not have the right to *adapt* the faith — only to *keep* it.

The faith — *the faith of Jesus* — did not originate with us, and we do not have the right to modify it in any way.

The Name 'Antipas'

Revelation 2:13 says, "I know thy works, and where thou dwellest, even where Satan's seat is: and thou holdest fast my name, and hast not denied my faith, *even in those days* wherein Antipas was my faithful martyr, who was slain among you, where Satan dwelleth." The phrase "even in those days" is plural in the Greek language and indicates a prolonged period of time over which persecution commenced.

Antipas lived at the beginning of that period of persecution. The name "Antipas" is a Greek compound word. It is comprised of *anti*, which means *against*, and *pas*, which means *all*. When those two words are compounded, the name Antipas actually means *one who is against all*.

The use of this word can figuratively describe a person who is *against everything*. The world would describe such an individual as *antisocial, contrary, noncompliant, intolerant, narrow-minded, a nonconformist, inflexible, obstinate, and uncompromising*. Based on this description, some suggest Antipas did not really exist — that the name typified the characteristics of the early believers against the backdrop of the evil, yet popular culture. But as we mentioned previously, an early believer named Antipas actually lived and was horribly killed in the acropolis of Pergamum.

Some used this word "Antipas" to describe the believers in Pergamum because, according to the pagan view, the meaning behind *antipas* accurately described the new Christian converts. As a consequence of their repentance and faith in Christ, a radical transformation had occurred. When people came to Christ, they broke all contact with their previous lives and separated themselves from the influence of the god of this world. Because of this separation, pagans harbored suspicions about Christians and believed they were *antisocial, contrary, incompliant, intolerant, narrow-minded, nonconformists, inflexible, obstinate, and uncompromising*. Does that sound familiar to us today?

The life of Antipas can inspire us today to hold on to the name of Jesus and not to conform to the ungodly culture surrounding us. We must refuse to deny our faith. We must protect it, guard it, and hold tightly to it, even if it requires giving our life for the name of Jesus.

Have 'the Faith of Me'

You may be facing pressure today from family, friends, or coworkers. Perhaps the devil is driving you to become more compliant to those around you who are living compromised lifestyles. Jesus said to the church of Pergamum, "Don't deny the faith." And He commended them because they held tightly to His name. Jesus is the Originator of the faith. He is the Giver of the faith. He is the Supervisor of the faith. The faith comes from Him, and we do not have the right to modify it. Therefore, only two options remain: We can either *reject* the faith or *embrace* it.

The believers in Pergamum made the determined decision, "We're going to *kratos — hold tightly* to the name of Jesus. We're not giving up, and we are not going to deny the faith. We're not going to break our commitment."

And Jesus responded, "That's good because it is *My faith — the faith of Me* — and it is precious to Me!"

STUDY QUESTIONS

Study to shew thyself approved unto God, a workman that needeth not to be ashamed, rightly dividing the word of truth.
— 2 Timothy 2:15

1. Jesus commended the believers in Pergamum for holding tightly to the name of Jesus and not denying the faith while under the threat of severe persecution. Today believers are facing pressure to accept the cultural norms of a morally deluded society. Explain the truths found in Hebrews 10:23-25 as they apply to remaining faithful in your walk with God.
2. There are pressures in the world today to deny the faith. What pressures have you personally faced that have been in opposition to your faith? According to John 8:31, 32 and Ephesians 6:10-18, what weapons can you use to overcome these pressures?

PRACTICAL APPLICATION

But be ye doers of the word, and not hearers only, deceiving your own selves.
—James 1:22

1. Identify areas or influences in your life that tempt you to deny the faith. Are you spending too much time in front of the television? Are your friendships inspiring a closer relationship in your walk with the Lord, or are you being drawn away from an intimate relationship with Him? Talk to God about those influences and determine to hold tightly to the faith you have been given in Jesus Christ (*see* 2 Timothy 2:22; Philippians 3:10-11).

LESSON 4

TOPIC

Who Is Balaam?

SCRIPTURES

1. **Revelation 2:13** — I know thy works, and where thou dwellest, even where Satan's seat is: and thou holdest fast my name, and hast not denied my faith, even in those days wherein Antipas was my faithful martyr, who was slain among you, where Satan dwelleth.
2. **Revelation 2:14** — But I have a few things against thee, because thou hast there them that hold the doctrine of Balaam, who taught Balac to cast a stumblingblock before the children of Israel, to eat things sacrificed to idols, and to commit fornication.

GREEK WORDS

1. "my faithful martyr"— μ μ ϖ (*ho martus mou ho pistos*)

   "my martyr"— μ μ (*ho martus*): a witness summoned to testify in a court of law; the evidence or proof presented in a legal case; pictures a legal witness who was only allowed to speak what he personally knew to be true; depicts the personal insight that qualified a person to be a "witness" worthy of being put on a public stand for examination; was also connected to the idea of suffering because if a person was called to be a witness, he was required to be faithful to the truth regardless of any potential acts of retribution that might be carried out against him by those who opposed his witness or who wished to suppress the truth; when an individual was summoned to be a "witness," it was understood that it could place him or his loved ones in jeopardy; to be a "witness" required the highest level of integrity and commitment, as well as a willingness to sacrifice oneself or one's status to uphold the truth; it was a very real possibility that a person could pay a high price for being a *faithful* witness

2. "my faithful martyr" — μ μ ϖ (*ho martus mou ho pistos*)

   "faithful" — ϖ μ (*ho pistos*): faithfulness or trustworthiness; could be translated "the faithful one" or "the trustworthy one"; in context, Christ found him to be faithful and trustworthy in spite of the agonizing circumstances that challenged him
3. "slain" — ϖ (*apokteino*): to slay or to kill; pictures the abrupt taking away of a person's life — in other words, murder, execution, or mass killing; violent death; butchery; carnage; a brutal, grisly, and gruesome death
4. "among you" — ϖ ' μ (par humin): right alongside you, or in your very midst; Antipas was martyred in a public, visible location, where the entire city would have been made aware of this hideous event
5. "but" — (*all*): nevertheless; a transitional word leading from a previous thought into the next; indicates Jesus had concluded His commendations and was moving on to deal with serious issues concerning the church of Pergamum that deeply disturbed Him
6. "I have" — (*echo*): *I have*, or *I hold*
7. "few things" — (*oliga*): small in number; indicates only a small segment of the congregation was infected with the spiritual disease of compromise

SYNOPSIS

The ruins of the temple of Dionysus are located in upper Pergamum. This temple was filled with demonic activities — drug use, drunkenness, sacrifices, and all kinds of despicable practices. Christians avoided these places because this was where and how they had previously lived their lives. They had been completely delivered from this abhorrent lifestyle and were walking free, living separate, sanctified lives according to the teachings of the Bible. But there was a group in Pergamum called the Nicolaitans, who said, in effect, "We're living too separately. We're living too strictly. Pagans don't understand us. We don't go to their theaters, their bathhouses, or their temples. Maybe we should compromise just a little to open up dialogue between us so they'll accept us."

This mindset was referred to as the doctrine of the Nicolaitans in Revelation chapter 2, also known as the doctrine of Balaam. In Greek, the word "Nicolaitan" is a compound word comprised of *nikao*, meaning *victory* or *to conquer*, and *laso*, meaning *laity* or *people*. When these two words are compounded into one, the new word means *those who conquer the people* or *those who have victory over the people.* The doctrine of the Nicolaitans was a doctrine of compromise and brought defeat to the people of God. Whenever God's people compromise their faith, they lose. They lose power. They lose holiness. They lose victory. When God's people compromise their stand for God, it *always* results in their defeat.

Jesus loved the Nicolaitans. In fact, He died on the Cross for them. But He *hated* their teachings and doctrines.

Like Jesus, we need to take a strong stand against compromise. We must walk in love toward those around us, but we must also walk in holiness. To walk in power, we must walk by a higher standard — and that standard is the Word of God.

The emphasis of this lesson:

The doctrine of Balaam — the doctrine of compromise — was seeping into the church in Pergamum. They were surrounded by demonic influences, and those influences were beginning to infiltrate the church. Where there had been persecution from outside the church, evil was now permeating this congregation from the inside. We are seeing the same doctrine of compromise attempting to work inside the Church today. We must be aware of it and stand against it!

'Even in Those Days'

As we have learned, Satan's power thrived in Pergamum. Jesus Himself called Pergamum "Satan's seat." Satan ruled there as the undisputed master of the house. In fact, in Revelation 2:13, Jesus made reference twice to the Satan's "seat" or *thronos*. Until the Church came along, Satan reigned supreme in Pergamum. However, with the birth of the Church in that city, Satan's stronghold became was threatened. And it's true that the task of the Church in *every* generation is always to unseat the devil.

Jesus said in Revelation 2:13, speaking to believers in Pergamum, "...Thou holdest fast my name, and hast not denied my faith, *even in those days* wherein Antipas was my faithful martyr, who was slain among you."

The Greek word for "even in those days," is plural and describes a series of days or a prolonged period of time. It depicts a time of persecution that seems to have been triggered by the death of Antipas. Because they behaved so differently from the pagans in Pergamum, the congregation in that city had not been looked upon favorably. But when Antipas died, a somewhat passive resistance against that church ended, and a very aggressive persecution began.

The only time Antipas is mentioned in the Bible is by Jesus Christ Himself. Jesus was so proud of Antipas that He called him by name. As discussed previously, the name Antipas is a compound word comprised of two Greek words, *anti* and *pas*, meaning *against all.*

When people came to Christ in the First Century, the act of repentance was such a defining moment in their lives — a moment that required total transformation and separation from the godless world around them. Unbelievers did not understand the separation Christians put between themselves and the godless world. Unbelievers judged Christians as being *against everything.* They were suspicious of Christians and viewed them as *antisocial, contrary, incompliant, intolerant, narrow-minded, nonconformist, inflexible, and uncompromising.*

Christians refused to go to the theater, and the theater was a very central part of life at that time. But they would not participate because of the depravity that took place on the stage. Christians would not attend athletic events because athletes performed in the nude. Christians would not go to the bathhouses because inside them, deviant activities took place. Christians would not enter pagan temples or burn incense to the emperor, which was viewed as unpatriotic.

Some believe the word "Antipas" in verse 13 is a term describing the world's perspective of Christians at that time, and that is true. However, an actual early believer named Antipas is memorialized in this verse nonetheless. Because of writings from Early Church fathers, we know Antipas was a leader in the church in Pergamum. Some allege he might have even been one of the early pastors of the church. We know he died a horrific death in the acropolis of Pergamum. He was martyred inside a brazen bull, probably bound with ropes, while a fire beneath the statue blazed.

Antipas, the Faithful Martyr

What happened to Antipas was gruesome, but when Jesus describes him in Revelation 2:13, He says, "*Antipas was my faithful martyr.*" The Greek reads very differently. It says, *ho martus mou ho pistos*, or *the witness of Mine, the faithful one.*

The word "witness" is the Greek word *martus*, which describes *one who is summoned to testify in the court of law or to present evidence or proof.* A legal witness was only allowed to speak what he personally knew to be true. This personal insight qualified the person to be a witness worthy of being put on the public stand for examination.

The word "martyr" or "witness" also conveys the idea of suffering. When a person was called to be a witness, he was required to be faithful to the truth regardless of any threat of retribution. It was understood that being a witness could place a person or his loved ones in jeopardy. Therefore, to be a witness required a person to have the highest level of integrity, commitment, and willingness to sacrifice himself or his status to uphold the truth. This "martyr" or "witness" was put on the investigation stand and interrogated.

Antipas had such integrity when it came to his faith that Jesus knew he could be depended upon. That is the reason Jesus called him "faithful." The Greek actually says *the faithful one.* It could also be translated as *the trustworthy one.* Christ found Antipas absolutely faithful and absolutely trustworthy in spite of what he endured for being true to his witness.

It is very possible that Antipas was the first believer to be executed in Pergamum for his faith. He was sentenced to be killed publicly. In fact, the Bible says in verse 13 that he "…was slain among you." The Greek means *right alongside you* or *right in your midst.*

The word "slain" is the Greek word *apokteino* and means *to slay or to kill*; it pictures *the abrupt taking away of a person's life*. It also means *murder*, *execution*, or *mass killing*, and it can describe *violent death*. One scholar says it presents the idea of *butchery*; *carnage*; and *a brutal, grisly and gruesome death.*

The City 'Where Satan Dwelleth'

That is exactly what happened to this Christian leader named Antipas. Jesus said, in effect, "It happened *among* you. You were all there. You saw it. This happened visibly, publicly. This did not happen somewhere in the corner, but right in the middle of town. And everyone knew about it."

Jesus stated that Antipas was martyred in Pergamum, where Satan's seat was located (*see* v. 13). The word "Satan" is the Greek word *satanas*, and it means *one who hates, accuses, slanders, or conspires against.* By using this word, Jesus was saying, "Yes, it happened in the same city where Satan is conspiring against you, in the place where Satan *dwellest*."

The word "dwellest" — *katoikeo* — in this verse described a place where Satan felt very comfortable. He believed he was the ruler of the house and, therefore, he could do whatever he wanted, including killing people like Antipas.

Satan was a real enemy to this congregation, but as horrific as the pagan persecution was, there was something happening to the church that was even worse than outside persecution. False doctrine was trying to develop *inside* the church. It was a spiritual disease being carried by members of the church. And if the infection was not stopped, Jesus knew it would spread to the entire church and affect the longevity of the church.

The Doctrine of Balaam and Its Infectious Reach

In Revelation 2:14, Jesus addressed the problem directly: "But I have a few things against thee, because thou hast there them that hold the doctrine of Balaam...."

The word "but" is the Greek word *all*, which means *nevertheless*. This verse could be translated, *"Notwithstanding all of these wonderful things that I said about you to this point, I do have something against you."* What did Jesus have against the church in Pergamum? Whatever it was, He felt it very personally. In verse 14, He said, *"I have...."* The Greek word for "I have" is *echo*, which means *to feel something very personally; to hold it very personally; to feel it very deeply*.

A false doctrine was being promoted by some inside the church, and the words "I have" in the phrase, "I have a few things against thee..." emphatically tell us that Christ was personally disturbed by something. The rest of that verse says, "...I have a few things against thee, because thou hast there them that hold the doctrine of Balaam, who taught Balac to cast a stumblingblock before the children of Israel, to eat things sacrificed unto idols, and to commit fornication."

After this church in Pergamum had withstood wave after wave of horrific persecution, evil was now lurking in their midst — an evil more deadly than the physical persecution they had witnessed. This seduction from inside the church was just as *dangerous* to the future of that church and to their effectiveness in that evil city.

Errant spiritual leaders who had veered from the truth were suggesting that the church begin to compromise their faith in order to coexist peacefully with the world. This mirrors exactly what some are saying today: "Just tone it down. Don't be so strict. Sometimes you have to 'go along to get along' with the unsaved. If you do this, maybe the world won't view you as so obstinate and unyielding."

Jesus was very deeply disturbed by this tendency to compromise. By using the Greek word *echo*, He was saying, "I feel this personally and very deeply." The dark path that these spiritual leaders were suggesting would weaken the church, diminish the influence of the Gospel, and hinder the demonstration of the power of the Holy Spirit. This suggestion to compromise was a spiritual weakness that would eventually weaken the entire church. Jesus called this mindset the "doctrine of Balaam."

Balaam was an Old Testament diviner who introduced compromise among God's people. As a result of his suggestions of compromise, Balaam ultimately defeated God's people.

Jesus said to the church in Pergamum, *"I have a few things against you."* The word "few" is the Greek word *oliga*, and it describes something that is *small in number*. This infection of compromise was not yet widespread in the church. Only a few had been infected by it, but it was beginning to multiply just like an infection.

An infection usually begins at a microscopic level. If caught early, it can be dealt with more easily and quickly. However, if not dealt with immediately, the infection that began at a microscopic level begins to grow out of control until sickness and weakness permeate the entire body. Jesus warned, in effect, "Right now only a few of you are infected, but if you don't take charge of this and put an end to it immediately, it will get out of control and affect you long-term."

Jesus referred to the false doctrine as the "doctrine of Balaam," and later, He will call it the "doctrine of the Nicolaitans." The word "Nicolaitans" is the compound word comprised of the Greek words *nike* and *laos*. The word *nike* means *to conquer*, and *laos* means *people*. "Nicolaitans" describes *those who conquer the people*. These people were inside the Pergamene church advocating a strange, new teaching that would suppress God's people and conquer them by eliminating the power of the Gospel, the Word of God, and the work of the Holy Spirit among them, which would have ultimately destroyed them.

The Danger of Compromise

That is precisely what compromise accomplishes. Compromise is fatal to the individual Christian believer and to the life of the local church. God calls on us to make the decision to have *no compromise* in our lives.

We live in a day when people are tempted to compromise their faith and to modify what they believe because of the changing culture surrounding them. The mindset of society is changing, and what once was considered morally wrong is now completely acceptable, even when it is contrary to the Word of God.

There is a *mass modification* taking place in the culture, but as believers, we are called to be different. We are not called to compromise in order to think and act like the world. The Word of God is unchangeable and so must *we* be as believers. Underneath the pressure to compromise our faith, we must yield to the Word of God and the Spirit of God for the strength to stand. Like Antipas, we can stand strong against the pressure and hear Jesus say, "Well done. You are one of My faithful ones!"

STUDY QUESTIONS

Study to shew thyself approved unto God, a workman that needeth not to be ashamed, rightly dividing the word of truth.
— 2 Timothy 2:15

1. Explain who Antipas was in Revelation 2:13, how he was martyred, and why Jesus commended him to the believers in Pergamum.
2. What is the "doctrine of Balaam," and why was it so dangerous to the church in Pergamum? How does it relate to today's modern church?

PRACTICAL APPLICATION

**But be ye doers of the word, and not hearers only,
deceiving your own selves.
—James 1:22**

1. We are surrounded in today's world by the pressure to compromise our faith in God and the truth found in His Word. Jude 1:4 speaks of ungodly people entering churches who say that living an immoral lifestyle is acceptable. List some ways you may have already observed this mindset. Find one or more verses that can combat a compromising mindset (*see* Romans 12:2).

LESSON 5

TOPIC

Balaam and His Doctrine — Part 1

SCRIPTURES

1. **Revelation 2:14** — But I have a few things against thee, because thou hast there them that hold the doctrine of Balaam, who taught Balac to cast a stumblingblock before the children of Israel, to eat things sacrificed unto idols, and to commit fornication.
2. **Numbers 22:5** — He sent messengers therefore unto Balaam the son of Beor to Pethor, which is by the river of the land....
3. **Numbers 22:6 (*NKJV*)** — ...for I know that he whom you bless is blessed, and he whom you curse is cursed.
4. **Numbers 22:7** — And the elders of Moab and the elders of Midian departed with the rewards of divination in their hand; and they came unto Balaam, and spake unto him the words of Balak.
5. **Numbers 23:8** — How shall I curse, whom God hath not cursed? or how shall I defy, whom the Lord hath not defied?
6. **Numbers 23:23** — Surely there is no enchantment against Jacob, neither is there any divination against Israel....

GREEK WORDS

1. "I have"— (*echo*): *I have*, or *I hold*
2. "few things"— (*oliga*): small in number; indicates that only a small segment of the congregation was infected with the spiritual disease of compromise
3. "against"— (*kata*): a forceful word that implies Christ would resist them until they repented of their deeds; carries a strong sense of domination and subjugation
4. "hold"— (*kratountas*): plural, present-active participle of *kratos*; a powerful grip and refusal to let go
5. "doctrine"— (*didache*): teaching or instruction that includes both the intellectual learning of a precept or principle and the applicable action taken as a result of learning that principle

SYNOPSIS

There was a group of leaders in the church of Pergamum who were believers to compromise with the world. They began teaching a doctrine of compromise, and Jesus referred to them as Nicolaitans. He felt so strongly about their detrimental teachings that in Revelation 2:15, He declared that He *hated* their deeds and their doctrine, also referred to as the doctrine of Balaam. The word "hate" is the Greek word *miseo*, which describes *a repulsion so severe you loathe or reject it.* Jesus loathed their teaching. He was repulsed by it because He knew when believers compromise their walk and no longer walk in holiness, they begin to lose the power of God. The fruit of the Spirit disappears. The gifts of the Spirit disappear. Compromise *destroys* a church.

God calls on us to walk according to the Word regardless of what our neighbors or society think. We are called to a higher standard, and that standard is the Word of God.

The emphasis of this lesson:

The doctrine of Balaam crept into the church in Pergamum, and it is creeping into the Church today. We must guard against compromising the purity of the truth of God's Word. We must be spiritually diligent lest we acquiesce to the lies of the enemy and the pressures of the culture around us.

An Attack From Within

Beginning in Revelation 2:14, Jesus says to the church of Pergamum, "But I have a few things against thee, because thou hast there them that hold the doctrine of Balaam, who taught Balac to cast a stumblingblock before the children of Israel, to eat things sacrificed unto idols, and to commit fornication."

The Greek word for "I have" is *echo*, which means *to feel something very personally; to hold it very personally; to feel it very deeply*. Christ was personally disturbed by what He was about to describe. He felt it deeply. What He was about to say to them was something He held very closely and very personally to His heart.

These words "I have" are very strong words in the Greek text. They emphatically express how personally disturbed Jesus was by the false doctrine that was being promoted by some inside the church at Pergamum. The church had withstood wave after wave of persecution successfully. Now, *from the inside*, the devil had launched an attack against the church with doctrinal error. It was seduction happening from within that previously bold congregation.

You might wonder how this wrong doctrine from a fragment of leadership within the church could have such a powerful effect on a body of believers that had already withstood such a brutal assault against their faith from without. But it was very difficult for the believers in Pergamum to resist these "inside" leaders with whom they'd had a relationship. These erring leaders had been with them from the beginning. These leaders were loved and esteemed, and it was therefore difficult for the church to stand against them.

Today's Church faces the same problem. Some leaders are in error — that is simply a fact. They have strayed from God's Word, and others simply try to overlook it. They might say, for example, "Well, we love them, and they love us. We know their intentions are good. They come from such a good family. They've been with us such a long time." They "dismiss" the error because they don't want to stand against those they love.

Similarly, it is very difficult to resist erring leaders who have been with us a long time and are greatly esteemed. Yet if the wayward leaders in Pergamum were not stopped, Jesus knew their teaching would eventually begin to spread throughout the entire church and would have a catastrophic effect on that entire body of believers.

How the Holy Spirit Corrects Us and Why We're Warned

Jesus made this important statement, *"I have a few things against thee."* However, "a few things" is not a good translation. This phrase was translated from the Greek word *ologos*, which describing *something small in number*. Jesus was actually describing the small number of leaders who had gotten off track. It was only *a few* — *ologos*. In other words, it wasn't every leader. Only a small number of leadership in the church had gotten into error.

Unfortunately, it was a very notable few. The idea behind this verse can be compared to an infection, which is initially so small that it's nearly undetectable. Jesus was saying to the Pergamum church, "At the moment the problem is *ologos* — it is small and easily treatable." That's the reason Jesus was calling on the church to deal quickly with the problem. Although the number of erring leaders was small, the wrong doctrine they were spreading was beginning to multiply like an infectious disease.

Jesus said, "But I have a few things against thee...." The word "against" is the Greek word *kata*. It is a very forceful word, which describes *a downward motion*. In this instance, it carries the idea of *domination* or *subjugation*.

Jesus was warning the erring leaders of the church, "If you don't repent — if you do not deal with this error correctly — I will deal with you. I will come against you; I will dominate you. I will subjugate you." This reveals that Jesus does not tolerate — overlook — those who propagate false doctrine inside the church. If repentance was not forthcoming, Christ would conquer this situation by extracting these erring leaders from their influential positions. Jesus was ready to surgically extract those who would not repent, and He would do it with "...the sharp sword with two edges" (*see* v. 12).

Jesus loved those leaders, but He would not allow them to pollute and defile the entire church. If those leaders were unwilling to submit to His authority and to self-correct themselves, Jesus would extract them. He would come with a sword, not to wound, but to heal and cleanse the entire church congregation. And Jesus is still extracting erring leaders today.

In Revelation 2:14, Jesus said to the church in Pergamum, "…I have a few things against thee, because thou hast there them that *hold* the doctrine of Balaam…."

The word "hold" is the Greek word *kratos*. We explored this word in Lesson 4, but in this usage, the meaning of "hold" connotes something negative. It is the plural present active participle, which means it describes *a powerful grip* with which the leaders in Pergamum were *holding tightly* to their compromise and *continually refusing to let it go*! The only reason Jesus would use this word *kratos* is, He had already warned them to let go. He had already corrected them, yet they continued to hold on tightly to the poison of compromise that was infiltrating the church.

The Holy Spirit works in the same way today. He corrects us personally, in our consciences. He corrects us through the Word of God. He even corrects us through the voices of godly leaders and loved ones around us. Jesus, along with the Holy Spirit, had tried to correct these leaders in Pergamum. But instead of repenting and surrendering, they continued to hold on to the doctrine of Balaam. They refused to submit to the authority of Christ, instead deciding they would continue as they had been going.

Though those leaders may not have used these exact words, they deliberately made the decision, "We will continue with our modification of the faith. We will continue accommodating the pagan world around us. We *need* to bend a little and compromise with the culture around us, and we will continue to do so!" They completely rejected the voice of Christ and held tightly to the doctrine of Balaam, refusing to bend concerning what Christ had already corrected them about.

What *Was* the Doctrine of Balaam?

In Revelation 2:14, Jesus refers to "them that hold the *doctrine* of Balaam." The word "doctrine" is the Greek word *didasko*. This is an ancient Greek word for "teaching," and it refers not only to *teaching*, but to *how to apply teaching*. It was the same word used to describe *a masterful teacher who would teach his knowledge to an apprentice*. This definition implies the teacher would demonstrate to the apprentice how to apply the teaching and put it into practice.

When the Scripture refers to "the doctrine of Balaam," it is referring directly to the information Balaam transmitted to King Balak in the Old Testament and how he instructed the king to apply the knowledge shared in order to destroy God's people. What is known about Balaam comes from the Bible and from other historical sources as well. Balaam was so well-known that even pagans and unbelievers wrote about him. In fact, the pagans wrote more about Balaam than they wrote about Moses! Balaam was very renowned in his time.

The Meaning Behind the Name 'Balaam'

The first mention of Balaam in the Bible is found in Numbers 22:5 when the Bible records that King Balak "...sent messengers therefore unto Balaam the son of Beor to Pethor, which is by the river of the land of the children of his people...."

What is known about Balaam? First, let's examine the etymology of the name Balaam. Three theories exist about the origin of the name of Balaam, and all three of them may be correct.

One group of scholars suggest that the name Balaam is a component of *Bil* + *'am* — with *Bil* referring to *the god Baal*, and *'am* meaning *kinship* or *relationship*. This portrayed the inseparable relationship between Balaam and Baal. In this event, the name Balaam would actually mean *Baal is my kinsman.*

Another group of scholars suggest the name Balaam is a derivative of *Bli* + *'am*. This seems like a small difference, but the word *Bli* in place of *Bil* causes a significant new twist to the name "Balaam." It means *without a people.* If this is the case, it explains why scholars struggle to nail down Balaam's national identity. This portrays him almost as a mystery man whose national roots are not known. This would mean Balaam was *a man without a people* or perhaps that he was *a loner.*

A final group of scholars suggest the name Balaam is from an ancient root meaning *to swallow* or *to destroy.* If this is true, the name Balaam not only was a name, but may have been a title that reflected his reputation for supernatural abilities to bring devastating ruin upon those whom he opposed.

When all three of these concepts about the origin of the name Balaam are combined, it suggests Balaam was a devout follower of Baal; that he was a man of mysterious origin; and that he possessed a widespread reputation for his ability to destroy his enemies. These three descriptions reveal much about the etymology of the name Balaam and about the man himself.

Who Was Balaam?

Most knowledge about Balaam is derived from ancient Jewish commentaries written by Jewish scholars from the city of Alexandria in Egypt. Alexandria was home to a large population of Jewish scholars and intellectuals. From their writings, much can be ascertained about Balaam. Some of these scholars recorded that Balaam was *a witch* and that he was *very wicked.* In fact, some scholars referred to him as "the wicked one." Philo, one of the leading intellectuals of Alexandra, wrote that Balaam was "a man renowned above all men for his skill as a diviner and prophet, who foretold to the various nations important events, abundance and rain, or droughts and famines, inundations or pestilence."[1] Philo describes Balaam as *a diviner.*

The intellectuals who wrote of Balaam had witnessed witchcraft as a common practice in Alexandria. They understood Egyptian witchcraft because they had observed cultic practices and rituals of the occult as a normal part of daily life there. For these scholars to label Balaam as a diviner was very significant. Because of their understanding of witchcraft and the occult, they would have never misused this word. They accurately described and understood that Balaam was a witch.

The most famous Jewish historian of all was Josephus, and he wrote that Balaam was among the greatest of the prophets at that time. This is a remarkable statement since Balaam lived concurrently with Moses. While Moses was an instrument of the power of God during this time, Balaam was an instrument of the powers of darkness.

In both the writings of Philo and Josephus, the word "prophet" should not be misunderstood. At that particular time in history, that word was used to denote one who was able to foresee the future. Even pagans used the word "prophet" to describe anyone who was a vocal instrument for the spirit realm.

Other names for a diviner include *foreteller, seer, soothsayer, consulter of familiar spirits, enchanter, necromancer, wizard, and witch.* The meaning of the word "diviner" is *a voice through which the spirit realm spoke; includes mediums and the use and practice of clairvoyance.*

Numbers 22:7 also describes Balaam as *a diviner.* This means he was *a witch, a medium,* or *a clairvoyant.* Balaam was connected to the god Baal. He was not a prophet of God. He was a false, pagan prophet. However, it seemed he had the uncanny ability to sense and discern when judgment would come to a people or to a nation. The Jewish Talmud says Balaam could understand when divine principles had been violated. He also understood this divine judgment would result when those principles were not followed.

Whenever Balaam observed a violation, he would seize the opportunity to speak out a curse. Judgment would follow, not because of the curses Balaam had spoken, but because he had observed that a divine principle had been violated. This made it appear as though Balaam possessed great supernatural abilities to curse people or a nation. When the curse of God would come on His people for their disobedience, Balaam would claim the consequences were a result of the words he had proclaimed. He was, in fact, a charlatan, and there is no biblical evidence that he had any power whatsoever to curse or to bless. Balaam was an amazingly wicked man who seized an opportunity to make money from King Balak as well as others.

It is important to understand that the devil possesses no power against you today. Balaam could not curse the people of God with his words (*see* Numbers 23:8, 12, 20-23), and the devil cannot curse *you*!

Truth is very important. Society can fluctuate dramatically, but truth is truth. Truth — God's truth — never changes. When we err from the truth, Jesus has something against that. He feels it very deeply and personally. We need to stick with the truth, especially in a day when it seems people are veering from the correct path of biblical and moral absolutes. *The Bible must be our anchor in these turbulent times!*

Study to shew thyself approved unto God, a workman that needeth not to be ashamed, rightly dividing the word of truth.
— 2 Timothy 2:15

1. List the three possible meanings behind the name "Balaam."
   a. *Bil + 'am*:
   b. *Bli + 'am*:
   c. ancient root:
2. Some believe Balaam was a prophet of God. How do the writings of Philo and Josephus refute this idea?
3. Explain Balaam's character in light of Numbers 22:7.

PRACTICAL APPLICATION

**But be ye doers of the word, and not hearers only,
deceiving your own selves.
—James 1:22**

1. To help us avoid being deceived, James 1:22 instructs us to be doers of the Word and not merely hearers. Pray and ask the Holy Spirit to identify any area in your life where you may not be "doing" the Word. Search for a passage that will reveal the benefits of being a doer of God's word (e.g., from the lives of Abraham, Moses, David, Deborah, Ruth, Daniel, et al).

---

[1] Philo, De Vita Moysis, I.48.

LESSON 6

TOPIC

Balaam and His Doctrine — Part 2

SCRIPTURES

1. **Revelation 2:14** — But I have a few things against thee, because thou hast there them that hold the doctrine of Balaam, who taught Balac [Balak] to cast a stumblingblock before the children of Israel, to eat things sacrificed unto idols, and to commit fornication.
2. **Numbers 25:1-3** — And Israel abode in Shittim, and the people began to commit whoredom with the daughters of Moab. And they called the people unto the sacrifices of their gods: and the people did eat, and bowed down to their gods. And Israel joined himself unto Baal-peor; and the anger of the Lord was kindled against Israel.

GREEK WORDS

1. "taught" — (*didasko*): to teach, instruct, or prescribe; in Greek literature, primarily used to describe the relationship between a teacher and a pupil or between a master and an apprentice

2. "to cast" — (*ballo*): to throw or to hurl; carries an element of surprise
3. "stumblingblock" — (*skandalon*): a trap used to catch an animal
4. "before" — ϖ (*enopion*): within the sight of

SYNOPSIS

Pergamum was home to two big theaters, the upper and lower theaters. The upper theater was the steepest theater in the ancient world. It seated 10,000 spectators. During the First Century when the church was being established in Pergamum, this theater was regularly packed with spectators. Imagine 10,000 people gathered to experience a variety of presentations — dramas, poetry, and music — being performed on the stage below.

Prior to the performances, drunken priests of Dionysus would appear before the stage with a bull, an ox, or some other type of an animal. They would walk the animal from the theater and up steps to the nearby temple where they would slaughter that animal as a sacrifice to the "gods." When the people saw smoke billowing into the sky, it was a signal that the sacrifice had been made, the gods were pleased, and the show could begin. This practice was the equivalent of opening the curtain to begin a show.

For the pagans of Pergamum, this was completely normal and accepted. It was the culture in which they had been raised. When the show would finally begin, often very disgusting acts were performed, which were not suitable for private *or* public consumption. However, the people of Pergamum had grown accustomed to these performances. They followed and accepted whatever their culture dictated.

The early believers in Pergamum lived separate from the world, and Christ calls us to live a life of separation today. We are in the world, but we are not to be a part of the world.

Over a period of time, an erring group of leaders in the church of Pergamum began to compromise. They began to water down the teachings of the Bible and to promote a lifestyle of compromise in order to conform to the pressures of the culture surrounding them.

Believers today find themselves in a very similar situation, and the question must be asked: Do we accept cultural norms? If culture tells us something is "normal," do we simply accept it? The answer is that born again believers are to live by the standard of the Word of God. The Bible determines truth, regardless of what is culturally acceptable at any given time.

The emphasis of this lesson:

In the Old Testament, Israel was lured into sin by the practices of the culture surrounding them. They began their moral descent by entertaining what they knew to be contrary to the teachings of God. They compromised just a little at first, thinking it was harmless, but they ultimately found themselves immersed in the sin and practices of the ungodly around them. The Church today faces the same danger. We must guard against compromise in our walk with God.

Balaam the Diviner

In Revelation 2:14, Jesus referred to the "doctrine of Balaam" in addressing the leaders of the church in Pergamum. The "doctrine of Balaam" refers to Balaam giving king Balak, the Moabite king, a strategic plan to destroy God's people. King Balak literally became Balaam's apprentice in evil. As we learned in Lesson 5, Balaam was an Old Testament pagan priest. He was not a prophet of God, contrary to what many people believe. Balaam was connected to the god of Baal. The meaning of his name indicates he was possibly a kinsman of Baal and/or someone who was mysterious and a loner.

Philo, a leading intellectual in the city of Alexandria in Egypt — which was filled with witchcraft and sorcery — wrote that Balaam was a man renowned above all men for his skill as *a diviner*. Josephus, the most famous Jewish historian during the life of Balaam, also wrote about this dark prophet. Even today, Josephus is considered by the nation of Israel to be the premier authoritative voice, *besides Old Testament Scripture*, on Jewish history. Josephus wrote that Balaam was among the greatest prophets of his day. That is incredible since Moses was also alive at that time. However, Moses was an instrument for the power of God; Balaam was an instrument for the power of darkness.

Both Philo and Josephus labeled Balaam as *a prophet*, which confuses people because the word "prophet" had a different meaning in their day. That title was also used among the pagans. During that time in history, a *prophet* was anyone who was a voice for the spirit realm, whether a voice to the pagans or to the people of God.

The word "diviner" also refers to *a medium* or *a clairvoyant.* "Diviner" also describes *a foreteller, a seer, soothsayer, a consulter of familiar spirits, an enchanter*, or *a necromancer.* It also depicts *a wizard, a witch*, or *a voice through which the spirit realm speaks.*

Numbers 22:7 supports the idea that Balaam was a diviner because we are told that elders from both Moab and Midian carried a "diviner's fee" in their hands to pay Balaam to curse Israel. The *New King James Version* of this verse says, "So the elders of Moab and the elders of Midian departed with the diviner's fee in their hand, and they came to Balaam and spoke to him the words of Balak."

Balaam's Sacrifices

Ancient diviners used a variety of occult practices to see the future, but one common practice was to slaughter an animal, spread its entrails on an altar, and attempt to read the future by analyzing the scattered organs. Numbers 23 reveals that Balaam accompanied King Balak to multiple mountaintops to offer animal sacrifices before he attempted to curse Israel. Many scholars speculate that Balaam may have been attempting to read the entrails of the animals that he had killed.

The sacrifices Balaam offered as recorded in Numbers 23 were not sacrifices to God. This was strictly an occult practice. Balaam was so well-known during his time that Balak sent his emissaries nearly 400 miles to bring Balaam to Moab. Initially, Balaam did not plan to travel to Moab, but King Balak enticed him by offering Balaam a house full of silver and gold. Balaam took the offer and traveled the distance to meet with King Balak and begin the process of cursing Israel.

Since Balaam was revered as a great diviner and soothsayer, he was well-known and called upon often for his supposed abilities to curse or to bless. That is the reason King Balak said in Numbers 22:6, "For I know that he whom you bless is blessed, and he whom you curse is cursed."

Balaam Could Neither Bless *Nor* Curse

However, in spite of Balaam's reputation, there is not a single biblical record that confirms that Balaam possessed the ability to bless or curse anyone. According to the Talmud, which was an ancient Jewish authoritative text, Balaam simply had the unique ability to discern when God's judgment was en route to a person, a city, or a nation. Balaam had enough sense to know that when people violated divine principles, they would ultimately be judged. Balaam would assess a given situation, and if he observed a person, city, nation, or people were violating a divine principle, he instinctively knew judgment was coming.

Rather than call people to repent and behave correctly, he seized the opportunity to promote himself and would declare, "I'm going to speak judgment over these people." The judgment was already in motion because divine principles had been violated. Balaam had nothing to do with the ensuing judgment. He was simply able to predict when judgment was coming, so before the judgment manifested, he would declare, "I will curse this people," making it appear as though he was bringing the curse.

When the curse arrived, it looked like it was a result of Balaam's words. But Balaam was a charlatan, taking advantage of the situation. He possessed no ability to curse and no ability to bless. There is no evidence of that in Scripture.

The Bible records that Balaam tried three times to curse Israel, but he could not. Balaam lamented in Numbers 23:8, "How shall I curse, whom God hath not cursed? or how shall I defy, whom the Lord hath not defied?"

Balaam could not curse whom the Lord had not cursed; he could not defy whom the Lord had not defied. But Balaam refused to be hindered when he realized Israel could not be cursed. Instead, he traveled with Balak to the high places of Baal to make sacrifices, hoping a door to the spirit realm would open. Through an attempt at divination, Balaam believed he would somehow have the ability to bring evil upon the people of Israel. However, after failing repeatedly to place a curse on Israel, Balaam conceded that divination was no match for the power of God.

Balaam finally told King Balak in Numbers 23:23, "Surely there is no enchantment against Jacob, neither is there any divination against Israel…."

Although some allege that people involved in the occult have the power to curse believers, Scripture clearly teaches that no one has the power or ability to curse what God has blessed! Therefore, this reminder about Balaam should be an encouragement to believers that since one of history's most infamous sorcerers was unable to penetrate God's protective shield around His people, *Satan has absolutely no power over us today!* Those who are in Christ and are walking in obedience to God's Word are safe, secure, and sealed in the protective blood of Jesus. The power of that divine protection can never be breached by someone operating with Satan's powers. The occult has never been *and never will be* a match for the power of God that resides inside a believer. This is precisely why the apostle John wrote in First John 4:4, "Greater is He that is in you, than he that is in the world."

The story of Balaam serves as a reminder to God's people that Satan may be the god of the unbelieving world and exert a measure of power over them, but he does not have power over believers. What God has blessed *is blessed*, and this fact cannot be reversed.

Balaam's Stumblingblock

When Balaam realized he could not curse the people of God, he *still* did not stop! He took the next step and said to the king, in effect, "I can't curse Israel with divination, but let me tell you how we *can* destroy the people of God." Balaam did not want to forfeit the wealth King Balak had promised him, so he continued his attempt to bring about a curse on Israel. But instead of directly cursing them, Balaam devised an evil scheme, introducing an evil doctrine and guiding Balak in its implementation.

Revelation 2:14 states that Balaam "...taught Balac to cast a stumblingblock before the children of Israel...."

The word "cast" in the Greek is the word *ballo*, meaning *to throw* or *to hurl.* It carries the idea of an element of surprise. The word "stumblingblock" is the Greek word *skandalon*, which was used to describe *a trap to catch an animal.* The way this animal trap worked was, the door to the trap was propped up with a piece of wood. Food was then placed inside the trap. Then when an animal would enter the trap to access the food, the door would fall, entrapping the animal as prey.

The Greek word *skandalon* is usually used to describe an enticement to sin. It describes the devil luring someone into his trap of sin.

Revelation 2:14 states, "...who taught Balac to cast a stumblingblock *before* the children of Israel...."

The word "before" is the Greek word *enopion*, which means *within the eyesight of.* It is the picture of *dangling bait before someone to lure them out.* The trap Balaam shared with Balak was to cast a stumblingblock to bring destruction upon the Israelites. Numbers 25:1-3 records the event.

> And Israel abode in Shittim, and the people began to commit whoredom with the daughters of Moab. And they called the people unto the sacrifices of their gods: and the people did eat, and bowed down to their gods. And Israel joined himself unto Baal-Peor: and the anger of the lord was kindled against Israel.

The Moabite women had, in effect, paraded themselves naked in front of the men of Israel who had not seen their wives or families for a very long time. They began dangling themselves like bait before the men of Israel, and the men started to lust after these pagan women. The men first began to simply *consider* surrendering to the temptation and compromising their godly standards until they finally took the bait completely. Once the women conquered them through lust, they led the men to the altar of Baal-Peor, which was a profane place of worship on the mountaintop. It was certainly not a place where God's people should be.

It is important to examine the progression into sin.

Israel's Progression Into Sin

1. The pagan women lured the men of Israel to perform sacrifices to their gods — ***the men lowered their standards.***
2. The men ate what they should not eat — ***Israel entertained what was evil.***
3. Israel bowed down to pagan gods — ***they accommodated what God despised.***
4. Israel joined himself to Baal-Peor — ***they entered into moral and sexual defilement.***
5. The anger of the Lord was kindled against Israel — ***they incurred judgment.***

What we entertain in our thoughts, we will eventually actively participate in. What we get close to, we will eventually take part in. Israel came close to their pagan neighbors and their ungodly practices, and what they had once considered reprehensible, they were now completely immersed in *and endorsing*. The result was, "the anger of the Lord was kindled against them." Their actions ultimately incurred divine judgment. They started with the compromise of lowering their standards of the uncompromised teachings of their God. Then they entertained what was wrong. Their quick descent into sin and immorality ultimately resulted, *by their own wrong choices*, in divine judgment.

The Doctrine of Balaam in Pergamum — a Doctrine of Moral Surrender

This Old Testament account illustrates the doctrine of Balaam. It was a doctrine of moral surrender. This is so important because of what Jesus said in Revelation 2:15, "So hast thou also them that hold the doctrine of the Nicolaitans, which thing I hate."

The word "hate" is very strong. The Greek word is *miseo*, meaning *to detest.* The world was luring into sin the spiritual leaders in the church in Pergamum. These errant leaders had begun reasoning, "Why do we live so separate from the world? We need to involve ourselves a little more with the world. Let's not be so restrictive. It won't hurt to think a little like the world so they can relate to us and our message."

But Jesus knew if they compromised, the doctrine of Balaam would be implemented among them, and God's people would begin *thinking* like the world, *speaking* like the world, and *behaving* like the world. Jesus was so opposed to this thinking, He said, "This is evil."

Instead of holding up a righteous standard, these errant leaders in the Pergamene church were endorsing a mitigation of their biblical standards in order to mingle with the world. But the Gospel never gives us an option to live by the systems of two worlds — the world surrounding us *and* the church world. There simply is no option. Jesus calls us to a life of separation.

God loved the Church so much that He warned these false church leaders in Pergamum to repent. If they were not willing to self-correct, Jesus would remove them.

Hebrews 13:8 says that Jesus is the same yesterday, today, and forever. What He has done, He is still doing. Jesus is still the Head of the Church, and He loves the Church. Because He does love us, He is still calling people to repent. If errant leaders do not repent, Jesus will put a plan into action to remove them from their influential positions of leadership.

It is important to remember that the devil has no power against the people of God. He cannot curse whom God has blessed. He cannot defy whom God has not defied. There is no "enchantment or divination" against the people of God! Although the devil would like to convince believers he has power, he is powerless against God's children unless he can tempt them to surrender themselves morally.

In Jesus' name and by His power, we have been given absolute authority over the devil. We have the ability to unseat the demonic master of the house. We can unseat — *dethrone* — Satan's power. He has no authority against us because we are in Christ, sealed and protected by His own blood!

STUDY QUESTIONS

Study to shew thyself approved unto God, a workman that needeth not to be ashamed, rightly dividing the word of truth.
— 2 Timothy 2:15

1. What was the "stumblingblock" Balaam taught Balak to put before the children of Israel?
2. List the five points to Israel's progression into sin because of the doctrine of Balaam.

PRACTICAL APPLICATION

But be ye doers of the word, and not hearers only, deceiving your own selves.
— James 1:22

1. Every believer can be vulnerable to the attacks of Satan, but the devil has absolutely no power over him. Explain why this is true according to James 4:7 and First Peter 5:8 and 9. Identify an area of your life where you feel you've been attacked, and find one or more verses to meditate on and to hide in your heart so you can gain the victory in that area.

LESSON 7

TOPIC

Who Are the Nicolaitans?

SCRIPTURES

1. **Revelation 2:14** — But I have a few things against thee, because thou hast there them that hold the doctrine of Balaam, who taught Balac

to cast a stumblingblock before the children of Israel, to eat things sacrificed unto idols, and to commit fornication.

2. **Revelation 2:15** — So hast thou also them that hold the doctrine of the Nicolaitans, which thing I hate.
3. **Numbers 25:1** — And Israel abode in Shittim, and the people began to commit whoredom with the daughters of Moab.
4. **Numbers 25:2** — And they called the people unto the sacrifices of their gods: and the people did eat, and bowed down to their gods.
5. **Numbers 25:3** — And Israel joined himself unto Baal-peor; and the anger of the Lord was kindled against Israel.

GREEK WORDS

1. "to cast" — (*ballo*): to throw or to hurl; carries an element of surprise
2. "stumblingblock" — (*skandalon*): a trap used to catch an animal
3. "before" — ϖ (*enopion*): within the sight of
4. "Nicolaitans" — (*Nikolaos*) to conquer and subdue people; a proper Greek name that depicts one who conquers and subdues people
5. "hate" — μ (*miseo*) to hate, to abhor, or to find utterly repulsive; depicts a deep-seated animosity; intense hatred; repugnance; something objectionable; pictures something that causes one to feel disgust or repulsion; a deep-seated aversion; it is not just dislike, but actual hatred

SYNOPSIS

The temple of Asklepios was located in the bottom section of ancient Pergamum in the Roman province of Asia. It was a massive healing center called the Asklepion. Asklepios was the god of healing. People came from throughout the Roman world to be healed. When they arrived, they were treated by medical doctors and the priests of Asklepios, who attempted to use supernatural powers to heal the sick.

The temple of Asklepios was populated with sick people who had come from all over the world. Even great Roman emperors would travel to this temple to be healed. As part of the healing process, they would worship the god Asklepios in hopes of being healed. The temple was built very similarly to the Pantheon in the city of Rome. It was massive in size, elegant, and exceedingly ornamented. Believers in Jesus Christ would never enter into this temple. They had been delivered from places like this. When they were saved and washed in the blood of Jesus, they were delivered from these pagan customs and avoided the places where these customs were practiced. Believers understood that because of the demons operating in this temple, one entering such a place would leave spiritually oppressed. So believers shunned these kinds of places.

However, the Nicolaitans — a group of false teachers who operated in both Ephesus and Pergamum — were influencing believers to compromise concerning their stance on sanctification and separation from the world. They would try to influence believers, saying, "We need to relax our rules. Rather than live so separate from the rest of the world, we need to *befriend* the world. We need to go where they go, do what they do, learn to 'speak their language,' be more like them so they will be more accepting of us and our message."

The Nicolaitans strongly espoused compromise with the world, but in Revelation 2:6 and 15, Christ said emphatically that He was so against their deeds that He *hated* their doctrine. He did not hate the Nicolaitans; He hated their erroneous teachings and spiritually dangerous influence.

It is important for believers to understand the doctrines and the deeds of the Nicolaitans in order to resist their influence in the church today.

The emphasis of this lesson:

Worship is the intimate adoration of God and is a vital part of being a strong, vibrant Christian. When you worship God, His glory is released to meet your needs. He wants you to worship Him freely with your mind and your spirit.

The Aftermath of the Doctrine of Balaam

Balaam was a diviner who wanted to destroy God's people, but he had no power to do so. Once he realized he was powerless to curse Israel, he introduced a method of bringing destruction to God's people, referred to as the doctrine of Balaam. He shared it with the Moabite king, Balak. Balaam proposed luring Israel into sin so they would bring a curse upon themselves. He had no power to curse Israel, just as the devil has no power to curse a believer. However, through incorrect choices and sinful behavior, a believer can bring destruction upon his own life, and that's what Israel did under Balaam's dark, deceitful scheme.

As we learned in our previous lesson, Balak became Balaam's "apprentice" who was enticed by the dark prophet into following him. In essence, Balaam said, "If you do what I say, judgment will come on the people of Israel. They will incur wrath because of their own behavior. If we send naked Moabite women to the Israelite troops and lure them into sin, they will worship the gods of the Moabites and incur God's judgment upon themselves."

The Bible recounts the effects of the doctrine of Balaam in Numbers 25:1-3, which says, "And Israel abode in Shittim, and the people began to commit whoredom with the daughters of Moab. And they called the people unto the sacrifices of their gods: and the people did eat, and bowed down to their gods. And Israel joined himself unto Baal-peor: and the anger of the Lord was kindled against Israel."

Shittim was surrounded by a grove of trees overlooking a mountain, and on the top of the mountain was a temple to Baal-peor. Baal-peor was a horrific god involving sexual debauchery of the worst kind.

With Balaam's guidance, Balak cast a stumblingblock before the children of Israel. Pagan women called the Israelite men to sacrifice to their pagan gods. Tempted by the allure of the Moabite women, the men reasoned, "What will it hurt if we lower our standards just a little? God will understand. We haven't been home for a long time, and our wives are far away."

The Israelite men eventually followed the women into the temple of Baal-peor. It was a place of sin that was diametrically opposed to everything their holy God had commanded them. When Israel entered that temple, they began to eat what they were commanded by God not to eat. The Bible also says they bowed down to the Moabite gods. Under a strong delusion, God's people literally bent their wills and beliefs to accommodate what *they* wanted to do. Numbers 25:3 states, "And Israel joined himself to Baal-peor. And the anger of the Lord was kindled against Israel."

Balaam's doctrine was synonymous with moral surrender. If Israel had refused to participate, this doctrine would have been ineffective and would have possessed no power against them whatsoever. But because the people of Israel listened and ultimately compromised, they incurred judgment upon themselves. Moral laxness and surrender resulted in divine punishment for Israel.

God has called us out of darkness. He knows that skirting around the edge of a darkened worldly culture is not the way to flourish. Accommodation to the world was devastating to God's people then, and it is devastating to His people today.

The Doctrine of the Nicolaitans

Jesus declared to the leaders in the church of Pergamum in Revelation 2:15, "So hast thou also them that hold the doctrine of the Nicolaitans which thing I hate." The word "hold" is the Greek word indicating *they were holding onto; they were refusing to let go of.* Using this word lets us know that Christ had already tried to correct them, but they refused to submit to His correction. They stubbornly held to their doctrine of moral surrender. Jesus was fully aware of the insidious plan festering inside the church and He *hated* it. Jesus loves everyone, including the Nicolaitans — but He hated what they were doing. Jesus loved them; He died and was raised from the dead for them. When Jesus shed His blood, He shed His blood for the Nicolaitans as well as for anyone who is in error today.

We previously learned that the word "Nicolaitans" is the Greek word *nikolaos.* It is a compound of two Greek words: *nike,* meaning *to conquer*, and *laos*, meaning *laity* or *people.* When combined, those two words becomes *nikolaos* or "Nicolaitan," which means *one who conquers or subdues people.* As a group, the Nicolaitans were introducing doctrines and deeds that were conquering God's people and eliminating the power of God from their midst. The church was becoming spiritually sick and weak. The doctrine of the Nicolaitans was destroying the church for whom Christ died, and He *hated* that.

The word "hate" is *miseo* and literally means *to hate, abhor, or to find utterly repulsive.* This describes *a deep-seated animosity, intense hatred, repugnance, the strongly objectionable feeling toward something.* This feeling of hatred causes *disgust and repulsion.* This is not just "dislike," but rather outright hatred.

Jesus was completely disgusted with what the Nicolaitans were teaching. He had no tolerance for it. In fact, He was outraged by it. They were actually promoting the teaching of Balaam, which is in every way a doctrine of compromise.

In the Christian world today, there are spiritual leaders who, like the Nicolaitans of the past, are seeking a dangerous truce with the world under the guise of inclusiveness and compromise. Inclusiveness is a dangerous term. Many of these erring spiritual leaders once held strong doctrinal positions, but over time, they began reshaping their beliefs to meld with society's changing moral climate. In the process, a very different Gospel is being produced than what is contained in Scripture.

Listed below are four indicators that Nicolaitanism has entered the modern church.

Signs of Modern Nicolaitanism

1. No emphasis on living holy and separated from the world.
2. No emphasis on the doctrinal teaching of the Bible.
3. No emphasis on absolute truth or absolute biblical authority.
4. No exclusionary belief that Christ alone is the way to Heaven.

No Emphasis on Holy Living

Under the guise of inclusiveness, this view reasons that there is no need for separation between believers and the world. All viewpoints are acceptable, even if they are contrary to teachings and doctrines found in the Bible. Instead of encouraging lives of holiness, many modern-day church leaders are promoting a message that is more accommodating to the multitudes.

No Emphasis on God's Word

Nicolaitanism dresses itself in the guise of progressiveness. There is no emphasis placed on the doctrinal teachings of the Bible. Instead, much of the doctrine is dismissed as being too restrictive or too exclusive of the beliefs of others. Instead of being deemed the absolute truth, the Bible is used merely as a reference for illustrations, motivational sermons, and principles. It is not used to instruct in God's way or to let someone know that his or her behavior is wrong. This current trend is so rampant in the church that the basic tenants of the Christian faith are largely unknown by most churchgoers, especially those who are younger. *This is an infection that is raging out of control.*

Basic Bible doctrines like the virgin birth, the sinlessness of Christ, sin, salvation, holiness, and eternal judgment are almost completely unknown. Where Nicolaitanism prevails, doctrine is replaced with social action, social justice, and an appeal to mass audiences by making people feel better about themselves.

No Emphasis on Absolute Truth or Biblical Authority

Nicolaitanism cleverly disguises as open-mindedness. It purports that everyone possesses a piece of the truth. *Real* truth — the truth of the Bible — takes an inferior place in order to equally honor the beliefs of others, even if those beliefs are diametrically opposed to Bible doctrines. According to this inclusive, progressive mindset, everyone is right and no one is wrong.

Jesus hated this kind of thinking. It is an alarming statistical fact that more than half of evangelical Christians today do not believe in the absolute authority of the Bible.

No Emphasis on Christ as the Only Way to Heaven

Nicolaitanism also promotes tolerance. There is no exclusionary belief that Christ alone is the way to Heaven. This doctrine asserts everyone can discover his or her own way to Heaven. This belief makes Christianity merely one truth among many other truths. This is a pagan principle purporting that there are many roads leading to the same destination in the afterlife. According to this mindset, the belief that Christ alone is the way to Heaven is considered nonsense.

A recent survey conducted among the most Bible-based groups in the Church reveals that one third of young Christians today believe the teachings of Jesus, Mohammed, Buddha, and other religious leaders all lead to Heaven. This is another sign of Nicolaitanism — and Jesus hates it! These faulty beliefs result in a powerless, weakened version of Christianity, where sin is tolerated, separation is ignored, and the need for ongoing repentance is disregarded.

That is the reason Jesus warned in Revelation 2:16, "Repent; or else I will come unto thee quickly, and will fight against them with the sword of my mouth."

It is so important for the Church to recognize Nicolaitanism and be determined not to enter into this dangerous mindset. We must avoid this doctrine of Balaam — of moral surrender — and stay with the Word of God. We must not budge from truth. *Truth is truth* and it *never* changes, no matter what direction society is headed at the moment. The world will go in another direction, and as God's people, we cannot live in both worlds.

Jesus is *the* Way, the Truth, and the Life (*see* John 14:6). That immediately puts us in opposition to other world philosophies. There is only one truth. As Christians, we must be committed to the teaching of the Word of God, and just as Jesus commanded the believers in Pergamum, we must *hold fast* to the name of Jesus and not deny our faith.

You may have friends who are beginning to meld their convictions with the world's in order to get along with those who live ungodly lifestyles. Pray for them. Don't be negative or judgmental. There is great pressure in our world today, but God has provided a way not to succumb to that pressure. In fact, He commands us not to bend to the influence of the culture around us.

STUDY QUESTIONS

Study to shew thyself approved unto God, a workman that needeth not to be ashamed, rightly dividing the word of truth.
— 2 Timothy 2:15

1. Explain the Greek meaning of the word "hate" in Revelation 2:13. Explain why Jesus feels so strongly about the doctrine of the Nicolaitans and its effect on the Church.
2. List the four primary signs of modern-day Nicolaitanism.

PRACTICAL APPLICATION

But be ye doers of the word, and not hearers only, deceiving your own selves.
— James 1:22

1. Jesus said in John 14:16 (*NLT*), "I am the Way, the Truth, and the Life. No one can come to the Father except through Me." Today's church is confronted with compromising philosophies. Many believe there are multiple ways that lead to Heaven. Explain John 14:6 and how it applies to the cultural pressures the church faces today.

TOPIC

Do Christians Ever Need To Repent?

SCRIPTURES

1. **Revelation 2:15** — So hast thou also them that hold the doctrine of the Nicolaitans, which thing I hate.
2. **Revelation 2:16** — Repent; or else I will come unto thee quickly, and will fight against them with the sword of my mouth.
3. **Matthew 27:3-5** — Then Judas, which had betrayed him, when he saw that he was condemned, repented himself, and brought again the thirty pieces of silver to the chief priests and elders, Saying, I have sinned in that I have betrayed the innocent blood. And they said, What is that to us? see thou that. And he cast down the pieces of silver in the temple, and departed, and went and hanged himself.
4. **2 Corinthians 7:9 (*RIV*)** — I don't rejoice that I caused you to feel pain and grief, but I do rejoice that my letter made you want to change. The pain you felt was your response to God's dealings with you.
5. **2 Corinthians 7:9 (*NKJV*)** — Now I rejoice, not that you were made sorry, but that your sorrow led to repentance. For you were made sorry in a godly manner, that you might suffer loss from us in nothing.
6. **2 Corinthians 7:11 (*NKJV*)** — For observe this very thing, that you sorrowed in a godly manner: What diligence it produced in you, what clearing of yourselves, what indignation, what fear, what vehement desire, what zeal, what vindication! In all things you proved yourselves to be clear in this matter.

GREEK WORDS

1. "hate" — **μ** (*miseo*): to hate, to abhor, or to find utterly repulsive; depicts a deep-seated animosity; intense hatred; repugnance; something objectionable; pictures something that causes one to feel disgust or repulsion; a deep-seated aversion; it is not just dislike, but actual hatred
2. "repent" — **μ** (*metanoeo*): pictures a change of mind that results in a complete, radical, total change of behavior; a decision to

completely change or turn around in the way one is thinking, believing, or living; a total transformation affecting every part of a person's life, both inside and outside, resulting in a behavioral change

3. "always"— ϖ (*en panti kairo*): at all times; in every season; at every opportunity
4. "repented"— μ μ μ (*metamelomai*): grief, guilt, regret, or remorse
5. "sorry"— ϖ (*lupeo*): pain or grief

SYNOPSIS

The ancient city of Pergamum was an extremely dark place filled with temples where sacrifices offered to the gods. This city was literally overrun with demon spirits and pagan religions. But in the midst of this very oppressive city, the light of the Gospel began to penetrate the darkness. Although the church was viciously persecuted, it survived and even *thrived*. Physical persecution did not destroy the church, but eventually the doctrine of the Nicolaitans entered in. This mindset of moral compromise and surrender threatened to destroy the church in Pergamum *from the inside*. This same mindset threatens the Church today.

When the leaders of the church in Pergamum began to allow compromise to enter, Jesus commanded them in Revelation 2:16 to *repent*! Repentance is an important part of the Christian life. Jesus is still imploring us today to repent when we have an attitude or behavior that is contrary to the Word of God. Believers today need to know what the Bible says about repentance because it is a fundamental New Testament principle.

The emphasis of this lesson:

Repentance and remorse are not the same. This lesson will focus on the meanings behind these two words, the differences between their meanings, and why remorse is not true repentance.

What Jesus Hated Then and What He Hates Today

As we have learned in previous lessons, in Revelation 2:14, Jesus expressed His great displeasure in with those in Pergamum who held to the doctrine of Balaam — a doctrine of compromise and moral surrender that was weakening the church. This doctrine, synonymous with the doctrine of the Nicolaitans, ultimately weakened the church, and Jesus expressed His disgust with its influence in verse Revelation 2:15 when He said, "So hast thou also them that hold the doctrine of the Nicolaitans, which thing I hate."

When Rick and Denise were raising their three sons, the use of the word "hate" was not allowed in their home. If one of their sons said, "I hate you" to another, there were serious consequences because it was considered a serious offense to use that word in the Renner household. Yet this is the word Jesus chose to use to express His disgust for the doctrine of the Nicolaitans. Jesus didn't say He hated the Nicolaitans; He said He hated what they taught and practiced.

In review, the Greek word for "hate" is *miseo,* and it means to *hate*, *to abhor*, or *to find utterly repulsive*. It describes *animosity, intense hatred, repugnance, something that is objectionable or causes one to feel disgusted and repulsed*. It is *a deep-seated aversion*. It expressed *utter contempt, hostility*, and *intolerance* for something that was taking place. All of these descriptions for "hate" in Revelation 2:15 describe what Jesus felt about what the Nicolaitans were promoting in the Pergamum church.

Jesus is longsuffering, merciful, and always gives us time to repent if we have strayed from the truth. However, the Nicolaitans were not listening to His warnings. Jesus warned that if they continued to refuse to repent for their compromise, He would remove them from their influential positions inside the church.

In review of our last lesson, there are four characteristics of modern-day Nicolaitanism: 1) no emphasis on holy living and separation from the world; 2) no emphasis on the doctrinal teaching of the Bible; 3) no emphasis on absolute truth or biblical authority; and 4) no exclusionary belief that Christ alone is the way to Heaven.

The Need To Repent

In Revelation 2:16, Jesus addressed those who were in error: "Repent; or else I will come unto thee quickly, and will fight against them with the sword of my mouth."

Many today do not believe Christians ever need to repent, but this verse clearly reveals that it is important to Jesus. In fact, when Jesus addressed each of the seven churches found in the book of Revelation, He commanded five of the seven *to repent*.

The word "repent" in this verse is the Greek word *metanoeo* and describes *a change of mind resulting in a complete radical total change in behavior.* It portrays *a decision to completely change or turn around in the way one is thinking, believing, or living.* Repentance is not based on emotion; it is a decision, which means we do not need to depend on our emotions to repent. Repentance may be accompanied by emotion, but emotion is not a requirement for repentance to occur. The act of repentance occurs when a decision is made to align oneself with God's Word instead of going his own way. When this occurs, a total transformation takes place that will affect every part of a person's life. Furthermore, this transformation on the inside will ultimately result in a change of behavior on the outside.

When Jesus spoke to the erring leaders in Pergamum and commanded them to repent, He was telling them to make a behavioral and doctrinal change in the way they were living and in what they were teaching. He was commanding them to repent and go in a different direction.

Is Remorse the Same as Repentance?

Most believe the words "repent" and "remorse" have the same meaning, but they do not. The word "remorse" has a completely different meaning from "repent" in the Greek language. The Greek word for "remorse" is *metamelomai* meaning *to regret.* It describes *grief, guilt, regret*, or *remorse.*

An example illustrating this Greek word is found in Matthew 27:3-5:

> Then Judas, which had betrayed him, when he saw that he was condemned, repented himself, and brought again the thirty pieces of silver to the chief priests and elders, Saying, I have sinned in that I have betrayed the innocent blood. And they said, What is that to us? see thou to that. And he cast down the pieces of silver in the temple, and departed, and went and hanged himself.

Although it may appear in this verse as though Judas "repented" for betraying Jesus, he did not. The Greek word *metamelomai* is used for "repented" in this instance. Instead of truly repenting, Judas felt guilt and remorse for his actions. When someone repents in the biblical sense — when he decides to make *a change of mind resulting in a complete, radical, total change in behavior* — the outward change that results is positive, not negative.

The fruit of true repentance is a change in behavior. But the Bible tells us that Judas committed suicide, and this is not the fruit of true repentance. It would not be typical behavior for someone who has truly repented to take his own life. But this passage states, "...When he [Judas] saw that he was condemned, repented himself [was remorseful and regretful]...and went and hanged himself."

Remorse — from the Greek word *metamelomai* — describes an emotion that grips a person because of a wrong act that he has committed. That person knows the act is wrong, yet he has no plans to repent and change his behavior, or stop his sinful activity. Like Judas, an individual can be gripped with remorse, but remorse rarely produces change in behavior. A remorseful person may feel guilty and ashamed about the wrong he has committed. He may regret being caught in a wrong behavior and facing the possible consequences of that behavior. Still, regret and remorse normally do not produce true change in an individual's life.

Because the word *metamelomai* is used in Matthew 27:3 to describe Judas Iscariot, it reveals that Judas did not repent in the truest sense of the word. He *regretted* what he had done to Jesus. He was sorrowful and understood he would lose the privilege of being part of Jesus' inner circle. Judas regretted what he had lost and was overcome with guilt and remorse. But he found himself in a position of focusing more on himself than on truly repenting and turning his life around.

Sorrow That's Godly

Although emotion is not a requirement for repentance, there are times when emotions can be felt by a person who is repenting. An example of this is found in Second Corinthians 7:9 when Paul wrote to the Corinthian church. In this passage, Paul used the word "sorry" or a form of it three times. He had corrected them for their behavior and said, "Now I rejoice, not that ye were made *sorry*, but that ye *sorrowed* to repentance: for ye were made *sorry* after a godly manner...."

In all three instances, the Greek word *lupeo* was used, meaning *pain* or *grief*. This verse could be translated, "I don't rejoice that I caused you to feel pain and grief, but I do rejoice that my letter made you purpose in your heart to change."

The *New King James Version* of Second Corinthians 7:9 says, "...For you were made sorry *in a godly manner....*" What did Paul mean by "in a godly manner"? The *Renner Interpretive Version* of this verse describes this way: *"I don't rejoice that I caused you to feel pain and grief, but I rejoice that my letter made you want to change. The pain you felt was your response to God's dealings with you."*

According to this verse, these believers were so deeply sorrowful for their misdeeds that they made a godly change in their lives — in their behavior and lifestyle.

In Second Corinthians 7:11 (*NKJV*), Paul states concerning their repentance, "...What diligence it produced in you, what clearing of yourselves, what indignation, what fear, what vehement desire, what zeal, what vindication! In all things you proved yourselves to be clear in this matter."

Paul was emphasizing in this passage that there is outward proof demonstrating that genuine repentance has taken place in the lives of believers. It's always true that real repentance produces indisputable transformation in a person's character and behavior.

STUDY QUESTIONS

Study to shew thyself approved unto God, a workman that needeth not to be ashamed, rightly dividing the word of truth.
— 2 Timothy 2:15

1. Define the meaning of the Greek word *metanoeo* in Revelation 2:16, translated as the word "repent," and explain who Jesus was addressing in that verse. Explain how the act of repentance applies to believers in the Church today.
2. Define the meaning of the Greek word *metamelomai* in Matthew 27:3, translated as the word "remorse." Explain why many Christians confuse the concept of *repentance* with *remorse*. Give one illustration of *remorse* and explain how it differs from repentance.
3. According to Second Corinthians 7:9, what is the evidence of true repentance?

PRACTICAL APPLICATION

But be ye doers of the word, and not hearers only, deceiving your own selves.
— James 1:22

1. Think about a time when you felt remorse but did not repent. Then compare it to a time when you truly repented about something. Explain the difference between those two experiences.

LESSON 9

TOPIC

Christ's Sword and Divine Judgment

SCRIPTURES

1. **Revelation 2:15** — So hast thou also them that hold the doctrine of the Nicolaitans, which thing I hate.
2. **Revelation 2:16** — Repent; or else I will come unto thee quickly, and will fight against them with the sword of my mouth.
3. **Matthew 27:3** — Then Judas, which had betrayed him, when he saw that he was condemned, repented himself…
4. **Revelation 2:17** — He that hath an ear, let him hear what the Spirit saith unto the churches; To him that overcometh will I give to eat of the hidden manna, and will give him a white stone, and in the stone a new name written, which no man knoweth saving he that receiveth it.

GREEK WORDS

1. "hate" — **μ** (*miseo*): to hate, to abhor, or to find utterly repulsive; depicts a deep-seated animosity; intense hatred; repugnance; something objectionable; pictures something that causes one to feel disgust or repulsion; a deep-seated aversion; it is not just dislike, but actual hatred
2. "repent" — **μ** (*metanoeo*): pictures a change of mind that results in a complete, radical, total change of behavior; a decision to completely change or turn around in the way one is thinking, believing, or living; a total transformation affecting every part of a person's life, both inside and outside, resulting in a behavioral change
3. "repented" — **μ μ μ** (*metamelomai*): grief, guilt, regret, or remorse
4. "I will come" — **μ** (*erchomai*): to come; to be en route; to be on the way

5. "to you" — (*soi*) directly to you; it means, *"I will come to YOU!"*
6. "quickly" — (*tachus*): indicates swift, high-speed movement
7. "fight" — ϖ μ (*polemos*): an organized and often prolonged military conflict designed to defeat an opponent; this is no mere skirmish — it is an all-out war
8. "sword" — μ (*rhomphaia*): a sharp, sickle-shaped blade affixed to a long pole; it was known for its long reach and its ability to cut through thick armor; its back-and-forth hacking motion, similar to a farmer using a sickle, penetrated the tightly packed formation of enemies

SYNOPSIS

Located in the lower district of ancient Pergamum are the ruins of a temple today called the *Red Hall* or the *Red Courtyard*. It was constructed with red bricks, and approximately 2,000 years ago, this building was the temple of the Egyptian gods Isis and Serapis. A large population of Egyptians lived in Asia at that time, and many of them lived in the city of Pergamum. There was a considerable amount of commerce between Egypt and Asia, and Egyptians congregated in these important Asian cities. This temple was one of the large temples where Egyptians gathered to worship.

In the First Century, believers would not enter temples like this because they had been washed in the blood of Jesus and had been delivered from their old pagan religions. How about you? Think of all the things you've been delivered from that you don't want to revisit in your life. For example, if you have been delivered from drugs, alcohol, fornication — or from *any* lifestyle of sin — you certainly don't want to return to that lifestyle.

Likewise, the believers in Pergamum had been delivered from all those pagan practices, and they shunned pagan temples. However, as we have studied previously, there was a group called the Nicolaitans in both Ephesus and Pergamum who taught, "We don't need to be so strict and 'separate.' These pagans are not so bad — in fact, some of them are good people. We need to spend time with them, accompanying them to their temples. If we befriend them, we have a better chance of winning them to Christ."

The Nicolaitans condoned compromise. Jesus was opposed to this, and He said He *hated* their teaching (Revelation 2:6). In Revelation 2:15, Jesus again said He hated the doctrine of the Nicolaitans. In both of those verses, the word used is literally "hate." The Greek word for "hate" is *miseo*, which describes *a repugnance for something*. It also portrays something *absolutely revolting and disgusting*. Jesus was actually saying, "This idea of compromise is disgusting and revolting, and I refute and reject it." Since that was the opinion of Jesus, it should be our opinion too.

The emphasis of this lesson:

Like the church in Pergamum, we are living in a time when the doctrine of compromise is trying to infiltrate the Church. Jesus strongly warns us today, as He warned the believers in Pergamum, to repent of compromise and to have an ear to hear what the Spirit is speaking to the churches.

Doctrine Determines Behavior

As we have seen in previous lessons, the teaching of the Nicolaitans had permeated the churches in both Ephesus and Pergamum — Jesus expressed His disdain for their doctrine (Revelation 2:6,15).

It is important to understand that *doctrine determines behavior*. If doctrine is based on the truth of God's Word, correct behavior will follow. If doctrine is erroneous, it will always lead to incorrect behavior. Jesus was adamantly opposed to the doctrines and deeds of the Nicolaitans. Doctrines and deeds are always connected.

Once again, the Greek word for "hate" in Revelation 2:15 is *miseo* and it describes *a deep-seated animosity, antagonism, or repulsion; a strong aversion, utter contempt, hostility, or intolerance*. This word also depicts *disgust* and *outrage*. Jesus was outraged by the doctrine of the Nicolaitans that had infiltrated the church in Pergamum. Those church leaders may not have been directly teaching that erroneous doctrine, but they were certainly endorsing it.

Believers must be careful about what we endorse. In the case of the group of leaders who were endorsing wrong doctrine in Pergamum, what they were promoting was utterly objectionable to the Lord. Those leaders were bringing a corrosive spiritual disease into the Pergamene church that was beginning to eat away at the church. Jesus was upset by this and expressed His hatred for it.

Repentance Is a Fundamental Doctrine

In Revelation 2:16, Jesus said, "Repent, or else I will come to you quickly and will fight against them with the sword of My mouth."

In our previous lesson, we studied the word "repent." It is comprised of the Greek words *meta*, meaning *to change*, and *noeo*, meaning *noose*. When these two words are compounded, the new Greek word is *metanoeo*, which means *a change of mind resulting in a complete, radical, total change of behavior.* This describes a *decision* — an act of the will. It is not necessarily emotional. True, Bible-based, repentance is a decision to completely change or turn around in the way one is thinking, believing, or living. It results in a *total transformation* affecting every area of a person's life, both inwardly and outwardly, resulting in *behavioral change*.

Repentance is a fundamental doctrine in the Bible that every Christian should understand. However, many believers today are confused about its meaning.

Repentance is a foundational doctrine of the church. It is still a responsibility for every Christian. To repent does not mean to be sorrowful, remorseful, or filled with guilt or regret. In other words, repentance doesn't have to be emotional in order to be effective. Emotion may accompany repentance, but it doesn't have to. Repentance is *a decision*. In fact, to repent simply means *to make a decision to go in a different direction*.

If you have children and you've ever said to them, "You need to change your attitude" or, "You need to change your behavior," you could have just as well said, "Repent," because it means the same thing.

When Rick Renner's sons were young, he and Denise wanted them to understand the biblical meaning of repentance. So when a problem with an attitude arose, Rick would tell that son, "Repent in your attitude." He wanted his sons to know they could make a decision to change. They needed to understand that when a person changed his attitude correctly, correct behavior or actions would follow.

When Christ told the leaders in the church of Pergamum to "repent," He was imploring them to change. In essence, He was saying, "I want you to think differently, behave differently, and teach differently." Those errant leaders were teaching compromise and inclusiveness with the world.

Jesus not only commanded these erring leaders to repent, but He also warned them about what would happen if they didn't repent. Revelation 2:16 says, "Repent, or else I will come to you quickly and will fight against them with the sword of My mouth."

What Did Jesus Mean by His Words '*Or Else*'?

Notice the words, "or else." The Greek word is literally translated, *"If not, however."* This phrase implies that Jesus believed those leaders would respond to His warning and repent — *however, if they did not*, He would have to deal with them another way.

Likewise, when Jesus calls on leaders today to repent, or calls on us to make a change in our lives, He expects us to do it, and He believes we will do it. *"If not, however"* — in other words, if we refuse to heed His instruction — He may need to deal with us in a different way.

Jesus was essentially warning the erring spiritual leaders in Pergamum, "If you do not listen — if you refuse to change — I will come to you quickly and fight against you with the sword of My mouth." The phrase "I will come" is the Greek word *erchomai*, and it means *to come, to be en route, or to be on the way.* Jesus was literally saying, "This is My signal. I am giving you an opportunity to repent. If not, however — if you refuse to heed My instruction, I will quickly be en route to you." Jesus was warning them that this was their final opportunity to repent — and if they refused, He would be on His way to them.

The words, "to you" in verse 16 is the Greek word *soi.* This is very emphatic, and it literally means Jesus would make a path straight to them to deal with them if they did not change. If they refused to heed His words, Jesus would make a direct path to them to personally deal with them.

Jesus warned these leaders, and a delay in His coming to them was not to be misinterpreted as His tolerance of what they were doing. If they didn't change, a time would come when He would come to them quickly. Similarly, there are times today when judgment is delayed, because God is patient. He gives everyone the opportunity to repent. Yet it seems some errant believers misinterpret God's delays as His tolerance of sin. But patience is simply not the same as tolerance. The Lord will eventually say, "Enough is enough!"

'I Will Come to You *Quickly*'

For Jesus to use such strong words reveals He had already warned these leaders and had given them previous opportunities to repent. But because they had repeatedly ignored what He had spoken, the opportunity to repent was coming to a close. Christ's warning was actually love crying out to them as He said, "You still have a few moments, a brief time, and I am pleading with you — if you don't repent, I will come directly to you, and I will come quickly."

In Revelation 2:16, Jesus said, "Repent; or else I will come unto thee *quickly....*" The word "quickly" is the Greek word *tachus.* It pictures *a swift high speed movement.* This word describes *Christ approaching them at a galloping speed.* It emphatically means the clock was ticking and time was running out. Christ was about to move at a very swift speed to deal with them because He had already given them ample time to repent, and this was their last opportunity.

Not Merely a Skirmish, But an All-Out War

Jesus continues in this verse, "...and will fight against them with the sword of my mouth."

The Greek word for "fight" in this verse is *polemos.* Most believers do not want to consider its meaning because it does not refer to a little *skirmish*; it refers to *an all-out war.* Christ was armed and ready to engage in battle if necessary, although that was not His desire.

Jesus was saying to the errant leaders in Pergamum, "If you choose to continue with these false doctrines, espousing worldliness and accommodation to the world, I will come swiftly and deal with you differently than I've dealt in the past. I will *fight against you*, and *it will be an all-out war!*" If Jesus is against something we're doing, we need to surrender to His dealings because we will never win in a battle against Him!

The Sword of His Mouth and a Message to Churches

Jesus stated in verse 16 that if He had to come to them, He would fight them *"with the sword of My mouth."*

The word "sword" in this verse is the Greek word *rhomphaia.* This was not referring to a common Roman sword. It was actually a Thracian sword. This particular type of sword had a sharp sickle-shaped blade affixed to a long pole. It was known for its ability to cut through thick armor with its long reach. The back-and-forth hacking ability was similar to a farmer using a sickle, and it could penetrate a tightly packed formation of enemies. Jesus was literally saying, "If you erroneous leaders refuse to do what I am lovingly warning you to do, I will come with a sword and hack My way back into the church that belongs to Me. The church does not belong to *you*; it is *Mine.*"

What a powerful, vivid description! Jesus is still speaking the same message to local churches today!

Jesus is the Head of the Church, and when anyone in a local church begins to lead that church in a wrong direction, if he refuses to repent, he is placing his position in jeopardy. If he does not change direction, Christ will "surgically" remove him and find His way back into His church.

In Revelation 2:17 Jesus said, "He who has an ear, let him hear what the Spirit says to the churches." It's interesting that Jesus said, "He that hath an ear...." Not everyone has an ear to hear. Not everyone listens when the Spirit speaks. Sometimes people are so involved in delusion and deception, they simply *cannot* hear. Jesus says, "For those of you who still have ears to hear, *listen!*" His message has not changed. He is speaking the same thing to the Church today!

You may be thinking to yourself, "*This has absolutely nothing to do with me. Jesus was addressing the church in Pergamum.*" But Jesus said, "He that hath an ear, let him hear what the Spirit saith *unto the churches....*" This message had application to all seven churches in Asia at that time — and to the Church throughout all ages. Jesus continues speaking these words to *anyone* who has an ear to hear in *any* age in *any* church.

Revelation 2:17 continues, "...To him that overcometh will I give to eat of the hidden manna...." Jesus will reward anyone who stays on track, even when faced with adversity. Jesus promises "hidden manna" if we refuse to veer from the message of God's Truth. Hidden manna provides us with everything we need in this life. God will bless us, not only eternally, but in *this* life! He will provide for us power, provision, protection — everything we need — if we will remain faithful to the teachings of the Bible.

We are living in a day when seducing spirits with doctrines of demons are working to lead people into error. It is well-disguised as inclusiveness, accommodation, open-mindedness, and being progressive in our thinking. The devil is injecting delusional thinking into society and, unfortunately, this thinking is also invading the Church. Some churches and church leaders are beginning to lower their standards. Even common believers are beginning to adapt the way they view sexuality, gender issues, and are entertaining thoughts that oppose precepts found in the Bible. This is a result of seducing spirits and doctrines of demons invading our world.

When Jesus spoke about the signs of the end of the age in Matthew 24, He warned that deception and delusion would pervade society. This is the day in which we are living. But even as the world chooses to go another direction, we as the Church must remain steadfast to the teaching of the Bible. We are obligated to hold fast to the name of Jesus and to not deny our faith in the teaching of His Word.

STUDY QUESTIONS

Study to shew thyself approved unto God, a workman that needeth not to be ashamed, rightly dividing the word of truth.
— 2 Timothy 2:15

1. Jesus warned the leaders in Pergamum that if they did not repent, He would come to them "quickly." What is the meaning of the Greek word *tachus* for "quickly"?
2. When Jesus declared He would come with "the sword" of His mouth in Revelation 2:16, what type of sword does the Greek word *rhomphaia* describe and what is its significance?
3. What indicates that Jesus' message to the church in Pergamum applies to the church today based on Revelation 2:17?

PRACTICAL APPLICATION

But be ye doers of the word, and not hearers only, deceiving your own selves.
—James 1:22

1. Matthew 24 reveals some of the signs indicating we are living in the end times. Included are descriptions of persecution, killing, and hatred against followers of Jesus. Also mentioned by Jesus is the fact that many will turn from following Him, false prophets will appear to deceive people, sin will be rampant, and the love of many will grow cold. List some indicators in the secular and church worlds indicating we are in those times. Determine to remain strong in the faith and to follow Him with all of your heart (*consider* Ephesians 6:10; Psalm 46:1-3; Proverbs 18:10; Nehemiah 8:10).

TOPIC

A Message to Overcomers

SCRIPTURES

1. **Revelation 2:12-17** — And to the angel of the church in Pergamos write; These things saith he which hath the sharp sword with two edges; I know thy works, and where thou dwellest, even where Satan's seat is: and thou holdest fast my name, and hast not denied my faith, even in those days wherein Antipas was my faithful martyr, who was slain among you, where Satan dwelleth. But I have a few things against thee, because thou hast there them that hold the doctrine of Balaam, who taught Balac to cast a stumblingblock before the children of Israel, to eat things sacrificed unto idols, and to commit fornication so hast thou also them that hold the doctrine of the Nicolaitans, which thing I hate. Repent; or else I will come unto thee quickly, and will fight against them with the sword of my mouth. He that hath an ear let him hear what the Spirit saith unto the churches; To him that overcometh will I give to eat of the hidden manna, and will give him a white stone, and in the stone a new name written, which no man knoweth saving he that receiveth it.
2. **Psalm 78:23-25** — Though he had commanded the clouds from above, and opened the doors of heaven, and had rained down manna upon them to eat, and had given them of the corn of heaven. Man did eat angels' food: he sent them meat to the full.

GREEK WORDS

1. "sword"— **μ** (*rhomphaia*): a sharp, sickle-shaped blade affixed to a long pole; it was known for its long reach and its ability to cut through thick armor; its back-and-forth hacking motion, similar to a farmer using a sickle, penetrated the tightly packed formation of enemies
2. "overcometh" — (*nikao*) Greek tense means one who is overcoming; a victor, a champion, or one who possesses some type of superiority; can be translated to conquer, defeat, master, overcome,

overwhelm, surpass, or be victorious; used to portray athletes who mastered their sport and reigned supreme as champions in the games; could also describe a military victory of one foe against the other; to be permanently and consistently undeterred in one's efforts to overcome and to obtain a lasting victory

SYNOPSIS

The Temple of Dionysus, located in upper Pergamum, was a horrific place filled with demonic activities that were regularly practiced inside. Drunkenness, fornication, deplorable sacrifices, and other unspeakable practices took place inside the Temple of Dionysus. Christians avoided this place because, for many, it had been their former place of worship. When they were saved, they were completely delivered from demonic worship. Now they were walking free of their former lives, living separate lives according to the teachings of the Bible.

However, there was a group in Pergamum called the Nicolaitans, who alleged that the believers in Pergamum were living *too* separate from their pagan neighbors. They reasoned, "These pagans do not understand us. We do not frequent their theaters, we shun their bathhouses, and we avoid their temples. As a result, we are alienated from them, and they can't relate to us properly. It won't hurt to compromise and 'meet them in the middle' so that they will accept us."

This line of reasoning, called the doctrine of the Nicolaitans, was referred to in Revelation chapter 2. As we have studied previously, the word "Nicolaitan" is a compound word comprised of *niko*, meaning *victory* or *to conquer*, and *laos*, which refers to *laity* or *people*. Combining these two words, the new word means *those who conquer the people or who have victory over the people.* The doctrine of the Nicolaitans was a doctrine of compromise that was bringing weakness and defeat to the people of the church in Pergamum.

When God's people compromise, they simply lose — they lose power, holiness, and victory. When God's people compromise the truths found in His Word, it will always ultimately result in defeat. That's the reason Jesus hated the teachings of the Nicolaitans. He did not hate the Nicolaitans, but He hated what they taught.

Likewise, the Church today needs to take a strong stand against compromise. We need to walk in love toward others, but we also need to walk in holiness. If we desire to walk in power, we must walk by a higher standard and refuse compromise where God's Word is concerned.

The church in Pergamum was assailed on every side by all manner of evil. Occult practices, including those in evil religions and government, surrounded them. But most dangerous of all was the doctrine of the Nicolaitans, which was the doctrine of compromise and inclusion. The influence of this doctrine was increasing in the church and was threatening to bring death to the church in Pergamum *from within*.

Christ strongly opposed this doctrine. He "hated" it and warned that He was coming with His sword to extricate it from the church if the leaders of the church in Pergamum did not repent — change what they were teaching and doing. Jesus also promised something marvelous to those who overcame the influence of this doctrine — *manna from Heaven*!

The emphasis of this lesson:

Jesus has called us to be *determined* to overcome. He has called us to be champions and to live victorious lives. Jesus promises "hidden manna from Heaven" — consistent spiritual nourishment — to divinely enable us to outlast adversity in this life. We simply need to "come to the table" and sit with Jesus as His overcoming ones!

The Unrepentant Will Be 'Surgically' Removed

In Revelation chapter 2, Jesus dealt with the leaders of the church in Pergamum. The doctrine of compromise and inclusion had begun to enter the church, and Jesus was calling for these leaders to repent. In His love, He gave them ample time to repent, but warned them that if they did *not* repent, He would come swiftly with the sword of His mouth. His high-speed advancement toward them would not result in a simple skirmish; rather, it would be an all-out war! He hated the compromise that was bringing death to His church, and He was passionate about removing those leaders from their positions of influence who refused to repent! With the "sword" of His mouth, He would surgically remove them from the church.

The word "sword" in Revelation 2:16 is translated from the Greek word *rhomphaia*, which was a Thracian sword, and it was the most feared of all weapons in the First Century. Roman soldiers dreaded the *rhomphaia* more than any other weapon their enemies possessed because it was essentially a sharp, sickle-shaped blade affixed to a long pole with the ability to cut through thick armor. With its long reach and ability to be used in a back-and-forth hacking motion, this sword was used by soldiers like a farmer using a sickle. It had the ability to penetrate the tightly packed formations of their enemies. Soldiers who held a *rhomphaia* would literally thrust their blade into the enemy and begin hacking back and forth. By using this Greek word for "sword," Christ was literally declaring "If these errant leaders do not repent, I will hack My way back into the church. The church belongs to Me. I will do what I must to retake the church for Myself!"

Jesus' message to the leaders of the church in Pergamum is the same for the Church today. He loves the Church and always gives people in error an opportunity to repent. However, if they do not repent, He will declare today, as He did to those in the Pergamum church, "If you refuse to heed My instruction — if you willfully choose to stubbornly do whatever you want to do — eventually your time to repent will expire."

Once again, Jesus was warning leaders to repent. He specifically addressed those leaders who were leading the church into error by encouraging a compromise of biblical standards in order to be more acceptable to the culture surrounding them under the guise of inclusiveness. Although it may not seem like it on the surface, this verse is an expression of the love of Christ. Jesus is calling out to them, giving them one final opportunity to wake up, shape up, and repent so they do not incur judgment. Jesus was issuing *a divine warning* to them.

He That Hath an Ear To Hear

In Revelation 2:17, Jesus stated, "He that hath an ear, let him hear what the Spirit saith unto the churches…."

When the apostle John wrote this verse, the statement was not unfamiliar to him. He had personally heard Jesus proclaim this. Throughout the ages, whether during John's time or today, Jesus has always looked for *those who have an ear to hear*. This implies there are some people who do *not* have an ear to hear. Some of those simply *do not want to hear*. But if we do have an ear to hear, the Spirit of God has something to say to us!

Notice again, in addressing the church in Pergamum, Jesus said, "He that hath an ear, let him hear what the Spirit saith unto the churches…." As we have previously discussed, the word "churches" is plural and applies to all the churches in the First Century as well as to churches of all ages, including the Church today.

Continual Overcoming Will Be Rewarded

Jesus continued in verse 17, "…To him that overcometh will I give to eat of the hidden manna…."

The Greek word for "overcometh" is *nikao*, and the tense is very important. It does not mean, "To him who currently overcomes." Instead it implies *continual* action. It describes *continual* overcoming.

God never calls us merely "to win a battle, only to lose the war"! Many win small battles, but lose the overall war in life. They are "hit and miss" in their efforts to seek God and walk with Him — in His Word and His Spirit — so that they can overcome life's challenges and obstacles that confront them. But we are called to be *perpetual* overcomers, to *continually* win in life's battles. The Greek tense of the word "overcometh" describes a person who *overcame*, who *is overcoming*, and who *will continue to overcome*. It describes one *who is in the process of continually overcoming*.

We are called to a lifestyle of overcoming!

This word for "overcometh" depicts *a victor*, *a champion*, or *one who possess some aspect of superiority*. Jesus has called us to be victorious — to be champions. He has called us to exercise superiority over the adversities of life.

The Greek word *nikao* can also be translated to *conquer*, and its implication is that there is something to conquer. It means *to defeat* or *to master*, indicating there is something for us to master or defeat. It also means *to overwhelm*, *to surpass*, or *to be altogether victorious*. It was used to portray athletes who had mastered their sport and reigned supreme as champion in the games in which they defeated all other athletes in the competition.

The word *nikao* could also describe *a military victory of one foe over another*. It means *to be permanently and consistently undeterred in one's efforts to overcome and to obtain a lasting victory.* So this word is not referring to a temporary victory. Instead, it pictures *a lasting victory.*

Finally, *nikao* can be translated as *to control, conquer, defeat, master, overcome, overwhelm, surpass,* or *be victorious.* This action of overcoming is what Christ calls every born again believer to.

Maybe you have had a low-level victory in a small battle. That's good, but you must not stop there. We are called to be altogether victorious, to master and overcome life, to defeat the odds, and to do it consistently to the end of our lives. In verse 17, Christ makes a promise to people who have a determination to constantly overcome in life. He says, "...To him that overcometh will I give to eat of the hidden manna...."

The church of Pergamum was involved in extremely intense spiritual warfare. They were standing for their very existence against forces from both the outside and the inside. And Jesus was calling on them to overcome. It did not matter how tough it was; His charge to them was *to overcome.*

That is Christ's charge to us today. And since Christ tells us to overcome, *we can do it!*

What About God's Promise of Hidden Manna?

What was Jesus referring to when He mentioned "hidden manna" in Revelation 2:17? To understand this phrase, we need to examine the Old Testament account of manna supernaturally appearing to feed the children of Israel every day in the wilderness.

When manna first appeared in the Old Testament, the people of God were undertaking a difficult journey across the desert wilderness to their destination. (Sometimes as we are traveling to our "destinations," the journey can be difficult too.) Their food supplies had dwindled, and they'd begun bemoaning the hardships of the journey.

Have you ever griped about your spiritual journey? Have you ever said, "Lord, this is too difficult. How long will it be until I finally arrive at the place You want me to be?"

This is what the children of Israel were doing. The wilderness was a huge expanse of desert that seemed to go on forever. They could walk a mile any direction and see only desert. If they climbed on a hill to see what was "out there" in their future, the only thing in sight for miles was more sand. Everywhere the Israelites looked, they saw desert. *Would this ever end?* They were tempted to feel abandoned, forgotten, and discarded — even though God had set them free from bondage, protected them from plagues, gave them water from a rock, and led them by "a cloud by day and fire by night" (*see* Exodus 13:22).

If we stopped to consider all God has done for us, how can we question whether God will be faithful to us or if we'll make it to our destination? The children of Israel doubted God in spite of all He had done for them. We don't want to make that same mistake!

An Open Portal and a Heavenly Supply

In Psalm 78:19 the Bible records that the children of Israel complained, saying, "…Can God furnish a table in the wilderness?" In other words, they were saying, "Is God going to continue providing for us? Will He be faithful? Will we really make it all the way to the Promised Land, or will we starve before we get there?"

What did God do in response? He is so merciful — He rained down manna from Heaven to feed and nourish them.

Psalm 78:23 and 24 says, "Though he had commanded the clouds from above, and opened the doors of heaven, And had rained down manna upon them to eat, and had given them the corn of heaven. Man did eat angels' food: he sent them meat to the full."

The "doors of heaven" refers to a heavenly portal. This phrase, "the doors of heaven" appears three times in the Old Testament. Every time "the doors of heaven" were opened, something magnificent poured down through them — something that came in superabundant supply. When God opened the portal of Heaven for the children of Israel, the manna began raining down.

You may wonder, *How much manna rained down in the space of 40 years?* Some rabbinical writings tell us that just one day's supply was enough to feed the children of Israel for 2,000 years!

When God provides, He does it abundantly! God was not worried that He was giving the children of Israel too much manna or that He would run out of manna in heaven. When the manna poured down from heaven in one day, it provided enough from them to eat for 2,000 years!

It is estimated that 65,700,000 tons of manna supernaturally appeared on the ground over the space of 40 years. Imagine if you woke up tomorrow and found tons and tons of manna lying on the ground, completely surrounding your house and entirely blanketing your city! How do you think people would respond? More than likely, scientists would fly in from around the world to examine the manna. Television cameras would come from every major TV network to film this event! Journalists would show up, and investigations would ensue. It would be a sensational, worldwide event if we woke up to tons and tons of freshly baked bread that suddenly and supernaturally appeared on the ground. It would be a huge event!

Committed To Overcome — Come to the Table!

This happened for the people of Israel every day during their wilderness journey, and the manna was used to replenish and strengthen them. In using this phrase "hidden manna" in Revelation 2:17, Jesus was saying, "If you will stay on track — if you will hold on to My name, continue in My teachings, and not deny the faith — I will supernaturally take care of you. Even if you feel like it is taking you a long time to arrive at your destination, with no real end in sight, I will be certain to rain down into your life everything you need to strengthen you for the journey so you can make it all the way to the end."

This promise is only for those who are committed to overcome! If you will be determined to overcome, Jesus promises nourishment, strength, replenishment, and the empowerment of Christ Himself. He will empower you with "Heavenly manna." He will provide supernatural nourishment. All you need to do is pull up to the table and sit. If you will simply come to the table, He will provide exactly what you need!

Jesus does not call us to succumb to defeat; He calls us to pull a chair up to the table! If we will come to the table, He will provide everything we need. He will provide spiritual refreshment for the tough times and all the spiritual nutrients we need to make it to the end of our journey. Christ promises to provide supernatural sustenance and replenishment for all who will commit to overcoming and to receiving from Him.

When Christ offered manna to the believers in Pergamum, He was offering them consistent spiritual nourishment that would enable them to forge ahead and outlast the challenges that surrounded them. That promise belongs to any believer who has decided to stay in the process of overcoming. That makes overcoming worth it all!

STUDY QUESTIONS

Study to shew thyself approved unto God, a workman that needeth not to be ashamed, rightly dividing the word of truth.
— 2 Timothy 2:15

1. Why was the *rhomphaia* dreaded more than any other weapon by Roman soldiers in the First Century? How does this description apply

to Jesus' attitude toward repentance by the errant leaders of the church in Pergamum? How does it apply to the Church today?
2. Explain how Jesus' call for the errant leaders in Pergamum to repent was an expression of the love of Christ.
3. Describe the meaning of "overcometh" — *nikao* — in Revelation 2:17 and the importance of the Greek tense used.

PRACTICAL APPLICATION

But be ye doers of the word, and not hearers only,
deceiving your own selves.
—James 1:22

1. You are on a journey to God's destination for your life. Like the children of Israel, it may seem all you can see is "desert" in every direction. Take time to remember and list some milestones along the way as a reminder of God's faithfulness in your life.
2. God promises "manna from Heaven" for those determined to overcome. If you haven't already done so, make a decision today to determine to be an overcomer. List some instances of God's provision — "manna from Heaven" — in your walk of faith so far.

Notes

Notes

Notes

CLAIM YOUR FREE RESOURCE!

As a way of introducing you further to the teaching ministry of Rick Renner, we would like to send you FREE of charge his teaching, "How To Receive a Miraculous Touch From God" on CD or USB format.

In His earthly ministry, Jesus commonly healed *all* who were sick of *all* their diseases. In this profound message, learn about the manifold dimensions of Christ's wisdom, goodness, power, and love toward all humanity who came to Him in faith with their needs.

☑ **YES, I want to receive Rick Renner's monthly teaching letter!**

Simply scan the QR code to claim this resource or go to:
renner.org/claim-your-free-offer

renner.org

facebook.com/rickrenner • facebook.com/rennerdenise

youtube.com/rennerministries • youtube.com/deniserenner

instagram.com/rickrrenner • instagram.com/rennerministries_
instagram.com/rennerdenise

www.ingramcontent.com/pod-product-compliance
Lightning Source LLC
LaVergne TN
LVHW020654100826
845148LV00012B/2487

9781680316179